HOW TO BECOME FOCUSED AND SUCCESSFUL USING THE 8 "S" TOOLKIT METHODOLOGY

"BECOME THE MASTER OF "YOURSELF" GAIN POWERFUL CONFIDENCE AND INFLUENCE OTHERS"

BY

LILLIAN COURTNEY (O'DONNELL)

DEDICATION

I dedicate this amazing book of knowledge to my parents who gave me life, love, music and knowledge. To my Father John Francis O'Donnell known to all as the Intellectual Snob (I was told this by a business man who said he knew every subject under the sun and people always went to him). He was a great writer and never followed his dream as he took the role of Father before his career. He taught us everything from Latin to maths to so many things we needed in life. His words were "if you have nothing nice to say do not speak"

To my kind and loving mother who taught me the piano and her love of music, poetry and Shakespeare. Her words were always to mind your character, you are who you hang around with and in later years to take care of yourself first so you can take care of your children. To my 3 wonderful children, Jonathan, Rebecca and Adam who have brought me into the 21st century mentoring me on new technology and processes. I enjoyed so much being a mother having the opportunity to stay at home and to be there for them when they came home from school. The joy of those summer days and just seeing them grow can never be replaced by money. Time with them was and is precious.

To my husband Tony who has had the patience in not spending time with me while I dug into writing my vision. For his kindness in always taking care of me when I was typing on this laptop and bringing me tea and dinner. To my sisters Eileen and Maureen for always encouraging and highlighting my talents. To my Grand daughter Marianna who will read this in later years knowing she gave me a new lease of life to put pen to paper.

I realise how precious time is and how fast it is going, I feel this book is urgent to get published.

To those who pushed me into the unknown when I was shy and on my way up through life and who made a huge impact on me, they will never realise their effect.

To Sr Kate (My childhood Teacher) she will never know how much she shaped my life both with confidence and for stage, I am forever grateful to her, for putting me on stage to take leading parts, for bringing me to the church to play the organ and pumping so much confidence and encouragement into me being a very shy child. For bringing me to the boys school to teach them our sacrament of communion hymns at 7years of age. I will in my life never FORGET her, as to this day I am in theatre and stage every week.

To Mr Linehan (Yoga and Psychology Teacher), R.I.P, to him I am so grateful for having introduced me to Yoga and the workings of the mind through lessons on Psychology. For introducing me to Dr Norman Vincent Peale's writings and the other greats. For showing me the opportunities out there waiting for me and always to get out there and grab them. He make a statement "Do not be a crustacean stuck on a rock, go out and swim the seas of life and take chances" I probably would never have traveled only for his encouragement other than I wanted to be a bond girl and live in Monte Carlo. Dreams do come true. I ended up in Nice in the South of France.

To Thomas Ni Callan (Choir Master) for trusting me with his choir when he went on holidays at 17 years of age and for introducing me to Professor Fleishman at University College Cork who in turn guided me in the direction of an academic music career.
(I did not take the opportunity due to having taught myself piano with my Mother on how to play and I believed most would have grades there if I had gone) but went to London to a great job in the Stock Exchange instead and trained as a contract dealer buying and selling Gold, copper and Iron Ore at the London Metal Exchange.

To Angela (not her real name) at CSA Agency for literally knocking at my door when I came home with positions at Apple, Measurex and FMC International where I met such amazing people. She introduced me to Sight & Sound college where multinational companies wanted dictaphone typists and telex secretaries with 80 words per minute. Which really stood to me in my career.

To Ellen Gunning (Irish Public Relations Academy). Ellen was and is just such an amazing lecturer at UCC, she made such an impression that I wanted to lecture no matter what. After years not having seen her we met up and she took my course on Personal Development for Corporates and put it into her academy in Dublin. She gave me unbelievable opportunities and introduced me to the top business people in Dublin. She is such a power house of a woman. I am so grateful to her.

To Dr Norman Vincent Peale, Tony Robbins who I trained with also and all the references I will refer to during this book. To all those at "The Tea at 3 Show" who sent wonderful messages and stayed for every episode. To The College of Commerce for taking my Programme into their night college and giving me the opportunity to grow. To all my colleagues in Toastmasters. To Laura at AJ&Smart for getting the ball rolling again.

To all my clients both personal and business for trusting me with their life and business directions and success.

There are no words that can thank you all so much for having been and still are in both my work and life.

On my creative side thank you to Marian Whytt. For her training in theatre and opportunities to take roles in her amazing productions. Her encouragement to put my poetry into one of her YouTube reels. She is amazing and always so encouraging.

To all the hotels and bars who supported me for the past 30 years always rebooking me on an annual basis.

To Pauline Hewertson from the UK. Pauline joined my Tea at 3 show from the beginning during Covid of 2019. I had this project in mind and I am so grateful as she kept sending a weekly message on how it was going. Even if you're a founder, leader of a team or oneself, everyone need that extra push.

Before I continue, before I forget, this point just came to my mind.

Who is the cog in the wheel of your life? Or, who are you the cog in someone's wheel of life, either in the past or now?

Answer here:- Make your list as far back as you can remember.

Finally to all who will read this book and take with them into the future, my heart, passion and love for my 8 S's method. To make the world a kinder, grateful and nicer place for all to live and work with confidence and peace of mind. To follow their vision with motivation, passion and creativity to project their talents. To guide others in what they have learned along the way as this is how we grow by sharing our knowledge.

My 8 S Toolkit can get you to work at your full potential faster and live the life that you deserve and were meant to live.

"A mountain can only be climbed step by step but you can also get ahelicopter".

Lillian Courtney

This book will speed up the tools you need to be just like that Helicopter. I am forever grateful to my family and everyone who are in my life. You must have patience when going through each chapter. Take a nugget of information away with you. Thank you for picking up this book as it will be the first step to finding YOU and INFLUENCING others.

There are 2 parts to this book and I really recommend you read the first part before going onto the 8 S toolkit to prepare the foundation before going forward. You can go straight to the 2nd half and still get great information.

CONTENTS

PART 1

Message from the Author..1
Introduction..4
Method for Top Situations..15
Chapter 1. The Brain made simple..17
Chapter 2. Value Graph with Exercise....................................35
Chapter 3. Mind-Body Connection...38
A True Story, The Power of the Subconscious mind..............42
Chapter 4. 4 Intelligences...48

PART 2

Chapter 5. The beginning of the 8 S Toolkit...........................53
Chapter 6. How to Find Your True Self…...............................59
Chapter 7. Self-Belief…...64
Chapter 8. Self-Confidence 72
Chapter 9. Self-Control 81
Chapter 10. Self-Discipline…..88
Chapter 11. Self-Value 97
Photo References 104
22. Conclusion…..112

I am so happy we are on this journey together. I am so grateful you took this first step in buying this copy of the 8 "S" toolkit. Love xx Coach Lil

Just a pic of me so you know who is chatting to you along the way. A picture paints a thousand words.

READERS NOTES

Why did you pick up this book?

_____

What do you want to get out of it?

_____

Write your old story here (Where you are now) write with pencil until the end.

_____

_____

_____

Which of the 8 S Toolkit are you hoping to Change? Pick it/them out now.

Self Awareness/Self Awakeness/Self Belief/Self Confidence/Self Control, Self Discipline, Self Esteem or Self Value?

_____

> Remember your old story as we will visit this subject in the end. Keep your answers here or in a safe place

With over 30 years experience in Multinationals and 10 years in the Coaching business, to be recognised at one of the top Irish awards in Croke park was one of the uplifting moments of my career.

What was the highlight in your career?
Besides family make a list below that you're grateful for.

MESSAGE FROM AUTHOR

The purpose and content of this book is to bring awareness of how we should function naturally in the world around us. How to communicate both in business and our personal lives. How to control and handle our emotions in a way that we were programmed to do so before being domesticated.

How important is my 8 S method for business leaders and anyone in everyday life to be successful? I, 100%, without doubt, stand by my belief from my own journey through life experiences and outstanding client results. I believe that with this 8 S Method it will be possible to live a balanced and successful life if and only if you follow the system I have designed.

Covering over 35 years of experience with multinational, government, organisations and the educational sectors, to my creative side in theatre, film and stage, I am humbled to have had the experience I have had in my life and with clients, to offer the 8 S Method as a recipe to reshape my readers to go and live a confident life. To reach their full potential, to use their talents and knowledge to also help others on their way up and make the world we live in today a more assertive, empathic and wonderful place to work and live in. To get the best out of each other and bring to light the talents that lie within those in business and life.

My end vision for this book is for my readers to find peace, self love, self value and confidence within themselves, to reach a higher level of thinking to go forward with powerful awakeness, confidence to be creative, innovative leaders of themselves with assertiveness to face all fears and to use every talent to rise to a potential peak at success on one's personal journey.

Rising their EI (Emotional Intelligence) to the level it was meant to be before modernisation.

To communicate with powerful self leadership tools to deal with any given situation. To be constructive not destructive.

I see so many Leaders lacking in EI.

All references will be credited; you may find some with "Annon".

I will not bore you with my bio so just google or LinkedIn me.

(Check my bio) I am an accredited ILI, Business & Personal Life Coach, ex Director at ICF. I hold the position of President at Toastmasters International Blarney, Ireland. I have a 2 year dip from University College Cork in World Development Studies and Certification in the study of the brain and NLP accredited from The American Union of NLP's. I have studied psychology and neuroscience from an early age and have read every book from the age of 17 in these subjects.

Attended training from top CEO's and trained with Global companies on facilitation (Jonathan Courtney, AJ&Smart, my Son) (Jake Knapp. Author of the Design Sprint) and Accredited with Team training on Design sprints and facilitation, Accredited also with certification for work/life balance with Tony Robbins organisations.
Trained by Tony Robbins himself.

Don't you just hate when someone is all talk about themselves it drives me crazy sometimes. In THIS case I need you to realise I have the experience and knowledge and portfolio for you to continue and get great information from this book. I could go on as I intend to continue studying until I die and could add certifications from Marketing Institutes etc here and many more but god that would be so boring, but you get the gist. I also have used all the education training and certifications and combined the experiences all together into one or more programs.

The study of human behaviour for the past 40 years has been my main obsession.

All above accreditations mean nothing unless one has the experience in all areas they are discussing, either personal or through helping clients to reach amazing results. This I most certainly have.

This is not EGO but I believe I am the Rolex and Rolls Royce accredited ICF/ILI coach consultant and among the top global coaches. If you do not believe in yourself how can you expect others too? LOOK AT YOUR VISION AS IF IT HAS HAPPENED.

The study of Emotional Intelligence, the workings of the conscious/subconscious mind and how we stay motivated with a plan to live a work/balanced life is essential for everyone to have learned.

Why? I have done not the 10,000 hours but the 100,000 hours with amazing results from clients. I rose, fell, rose, fell, rose and fell building my empire to where it is today. I have stayed up studying, sleepless nights, up at 5am to give workshops in other counties and countries.

Who said it was going to be easy? I am still climbing that mountain, sometimes with bare feet and stones sticking into them. Writing this book will give me the purpose and give me that excitement in the pit of my soul. I feel it will elevate me that extra step to the top of the mountain knowing that I shared my knowledge with you all. Hence completing the beginning of my purpose to the world.

There will be those who will praise and those who will or have knocked your ideas and stamp on you like a fly, I am telling you NOW to never listen and never give up if YOU believe in your vision and dreams, no MATTER how long it takes to get there. You will succeed.

So bare with me, wow, sorry for the self rant but I need you to realise I have gone through the eye of the storm to come out the other side to get here also. It is my first book and I am so happy you're joining me on this journey.

It is a learning journey for me also.

Skip to page 12 if you do not want to read on but I feel every word will help you along the way.

INTRODUCTION

Why my 8 "S" methodology?
.
A,A,B,C,D,E,V, L concept of Personal Development (Soft Skills)?

I came up with this simple concept combining the root cause of the majority of my clients, which was, an imbalance of work/life and their thought patterns all having to do with mindset and unawareness of the self. Be it top Ceo's to every walk of life. Within these 8 areas for 90% of those who attended my webinars, lectures and workshops these patterns seemed to prevail be it consciously or unconsciously to the client or attendee themselves.

This seeped into all areas be it work or life even though their craft and talents were there ready to be discovered. Having realised each area, we as humans are so similar. I myself would have been the self instigator of all 8 on my path to self awakening through my own experience and also studying people's behaviour around me through my coaching.

"Upgrade your emotional home" T Robbins

Live in a beautiful state, no matter what, life is too short to suffer.

Human behaviour has been a subject that has fascinated me from a young age. How our brain functions. Why do we do things opposite to what we need to do? I could go on. A book that changed my life at 17 given to me by my psychology lecturer. "The power of positive thinking" by Dr Norman Vincent Peale, it saved my life. Being a very shy person unless on stage where I came alive.

Having spent 10 years, on and off writing out several versions and titles of this book, having 2,008 live episodes of my coaching show online called "The Tea at 3 Show" (recognised by the national TV Virgin), 6 years of articles, 4 years of a coaching radio show, 4 years of a coaching show called "Dr Lil" on Irish Radio International, I was drowning in information, research notes and details and wanted to put everything into this book. It was getting so confusing with so many different versions that I believe it pushed me away from sitting down and penning this version up to now. It has now again whilst writing this line been changed to a simple hand book and may change as I go along to a full blown book.

Knowledge is essential and amazing but in my case it was getting dangerous so I decided to file away all the scripts, journals and get a blank journal and start fresh. I looked at the course I was giving at the College of Commerce here in the city which was getting high quality results for the students attending, be it business or personal areas, amazingly it had all the ingredients of how to be successful and live a focused life and it was all I had wanted to write but a different format.

"BINGO" I thought let's do this. I then got into a more confused state as this was a full 12 modules course. Can this be diluted into a morning or a day workshop? Will I put this into a book? A handbook or what? I then left it again and was on a training course in Italy with my Son Jonathan and Laura on the team asked about what I was doing.

I told her about my plan and she asked about it and I showed her the beginning draft. She asked when I had intended to complete it and I said March 2023. She said why not Dec 2022. I knew when you have family and a business things get in the way so I put March in my diary as the completion date. Will I reach it? I am determined. Guys it's November 2022 now. Let's see. Also my son Jonathan, he was really great as he used to say (and is still saying) that it will probably take another 10 years as I am talking about this book as long as he can remember.

December or March? It stayed in my mind all the way back to Ireland. I know if I am put under pressure I can do anything. Time is my enemy. The more time I have the less I get done. I work like a whale in the deep sea under pressure so opposite to so many.

In saying that **TIME IS YOUR ENEMY**.

I decided March was a better date for me to give myself a realistic timeframe. So here I am, back again, it's now April 5th, due to ending up in Hospital with a kidney infection in my quest to get this complete. I had been in such a brilliant flow and we never know what the next day brings. So I am still happy as I am halfway through and I am on my way to completion of a vision I dreamt of for so many years. Just to have pen to paper or type to screen is so uplifting. (Please start your vision) Who cares if you fail.

It's December how I just love Christmas.

December is a time for family and year end closing projects and reflecting on the year gone by. I am. Still on my way.

Sprint is the beginning of new life, let's have it complete when all the flowers and trees are in full bloom.

Hence I am not too far behind Spring 2023

(Note to you all, its Spring 2024 now finally getting to complete)

Let's run with our dreams…

I am ready with coffee and focused.

Believe you can and it will happen. Just take that first step.

Doubt, confusion with so much knowledge, scripts and such excitement.

Ok lets just do this, take the chance, people will love it or hate it but to me this is essential information, I am beyond passionate about these 8 S's. As I said above, I felt the Rolex of the industry, the Royce of my own craft, meaning "confident and I had this desperate feeling of urgency" to get my knowledge out there. Clients were endorsing this so I just had to do it. You may say it's ego but believe in yourself. Yes, people may hate this or love it but at least I will have put my thoughts on paper to share to the world and completed my purpose. I'm repeating words from above but I am writing this as I am thinking along the way and being my authentic self.

Again here I am, will I listen to my live videos?, Will I take information from my articles that are already there, why waste time? This aspect of the journey kept nagging me. So here I am off again with a blank canvas not allowing my crowded information to interfere with my thought pattern.

This is a GAME CHANGER for everyone so far so I thought let's just get this down once and for all.

I must say it takes peeling off a lot of layers of the onion of life to get to this state of peace and self awakeness.

I myself (another book) like all others in business or life will keep changing, re-inventing, updating my inner computer and knowledge to keep up with the fast speeding world.

We are now living in a time where you **must be awake, focused, motivated**, and **super confident and creative** to be successful for any other reason other than mostly for a self successful journey through life. You are either starting off
or slowing down in business or life but you need to be able to use the 8 S's method in every walk of life to live a balanced, happy and peaceful existence. Let's begin and go on this journey together. I am so looking forward to being your coach, friend and companion until the end. You can also pick out any of the 8 S's you feel you need to build first and go back to the others. I do suggest you chill and come along with me from A to V.

It is not a book you need to read from cover to end but can be opened in any given area you feel you need to brush upon.

Personally, I would commence at the beginning and keep this book like a bible of powerful self coaching tools to guide you in times of indecisiveness to build back momentum in any given area.

Happy Reading…..

SIT BACK AND ENJOY THIS BOOK…..

Recline your seats, sit back, you're in for one hell of a bumpy ride.
Yes, you heard me, that is what life is going to be in all areas of business and life and already is for most people but this book (bible for success) will bring you to self awareness, we will cry together, laugh together and come out the other end celebrating.

Nobody said it was going to be easy.

If you're lucky you have escaped the rapids of life or are either out at sea or drifting in circles or in the calm of life having learned so much from the ups and downs of the tsunami of life and business or you are starting out in life in all areas.

We as humans were more emotionally intelligent years ago than now. We had an animal instinct to survive, a sense of danger, we lived with nature until we became modernised. Personal Development was never discussed, or, did not need to be discussed as everything came natural.

There's a way to achieve great success and focus and this is through confidence in my writings, follow step by step my advice with unrestricted energy. You will soon be the master of yourself to achieve great things you were meant to achieve. Read every word.

This is not a book where you look through the pages or try to get the message from the back pages. It is kind of a **"Study Pamphlet"**.

Let's get going. I am determined to get you back on track or on to an amazing successful and peaceful mindset.

Remember take notes and highlight what is important to you along the way. This will help you look back later as we as humans will not remember as we take in so much information. It also keeps us alert to take notes.

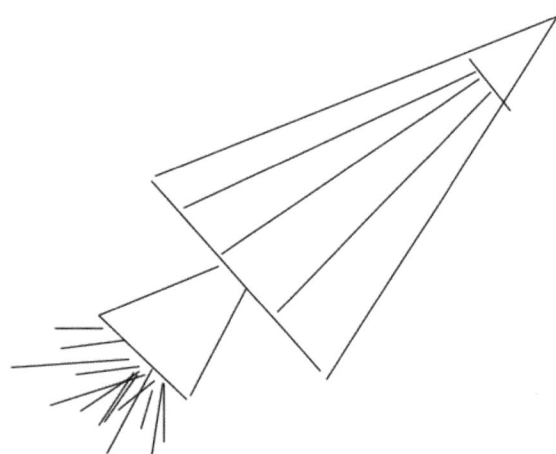

How proud am I having designed this on Excel.
Fasten your seatbelts and let's GOOOO…..

I have put together a method from top situations I have encountered with Multinational Teams, SME and personal clients and diluted these into 8 main areas to be more focused and successful to allow you to move forward in life under the headline of:-

SOFT SKILLS, Emotional Intelligence/Personal Development

. Self Awareness, Self Awakeness
. Self Belief
. Self Confidence/Self Control
. Self Discipline/
. Self Value
. Self Love

NB…..Under Self control **TAKE CONTROL** of your life. It is called "Self control" be in control of your life as so many allow others to take over the controls

"Use the powers that human nature has so lavishly dispensed to your powers which you are now allowing to rust". ANNON

Let's get down to business. Let's go inside and find that person you really are. We will peel off the layers of life and find that confident, creative, problem solving child full of potential that we can use as we go forward.

Remember these exercises have changed people's lives and businesses and shall do the same for you. This is now and the future. So let's get a new fresh journal and begin.

ARE YOU READY?

Ok Let's Go .... Ha! Ha!

The first step is to decide to be each S in our toolkit..

Read over above list

From now on we are going to get into this and it's the secret sauce for the rest of your life.

CHAPTER 1

THE BRAIN MADE SIMPLE

Before we delve into the 8 S method, I want to introduce you to the most important app you will ever need in life.

Your **BRAIN.**

Please continue to read.

It's not a biology lesson. I promise it is essential information you were never told in the educational sector growing up.

This is urgent information for everyone to know how they function. We all use the apps in our phones but so many do not know anything on how we function, how we communicate, how we control our emotions and thoughts. How we use the apps in our central control system, our BRAIN.

Your mind is the controller of all your emotions, thoughts, actions plus your state. It is the central computer that runs your whole life. There you see people getting healthy getting the 6 packs, swimming etc (of course this is urgent) but they do not know how their main app works. You see a percentage of people making all the money and having all the luxuries they wished for only to end up miserable.

You need to know how to function from a focused perspective and with awareness as a leader of teams or a leader of your life.

We need to modernise our brain to function in this new modern world. To be creative, innovative, yes, but imagine knowing how to use the apps in one's brain, how this level of innovation and creativity would rise for oneself, teams, company production and profits also.

Please stick with me on this journey. You can of course go to the 8th S tool kit but I really believe this will change the way you think going forward.

I believe we have 3 brains.

2 have been proven.

The Brain and Stomach.

Neurons have been found in the stomach but to me I believe our heart also has its own mind. Look at people in love, the stomach (gut) is their rudder telling them the correct direction but the heart takes over. Did you ever say I have a gut feeling, well that is always correct and your FIRST decision is always the correct one?

Hold on I found this on google: -

In 1991, it was discovered that the heart has its "little brain" or "intrinsic cardiac nervous system." This "heart brain" is composed of approximately 40,000 neurons that are alike neurons in the brain, meaning that the heart has its own nervous system.Author "Armour"

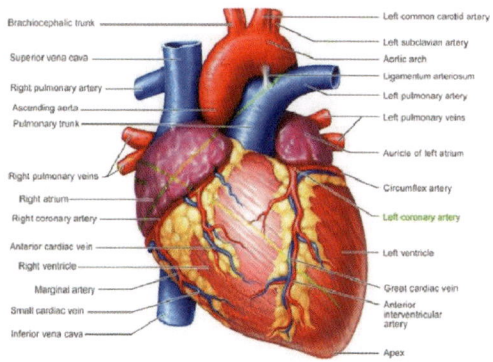

40,000 Neurons like the brain. It has its own nervous system. It thinks for itself.

Does your stomach have a memory?

Our gut has the ability to learn behaviour thanks to the network of neurons within the wall of the gastrointestinal tract. Interestingly, learning and memory processes take part in the gut.

(Taken from notes)

"I have a memory"

So, this was just to let you know not only does your Brain have neurons, but your gut and heart also do.

Let's get back to business and discuss your BRAIN on layman's terms..

The most important app you need to know about. I know you want to get onto the 8'S tool kit therefore, I will not delve deeply into this subject but just what you really need to know as a human being going through life. It is so important to have tools to control all emotions and face decisions or any given situation that comes up throughout your journey.

Brain facts: -

It weighs 3 pounds (lbs)
It uses 20% of your energy daily. It has 80 -100 Billion Brain cells
Each one of these has 1-10,000 connections each.
More connections than the stars.

You literally have miles of wiring that it could reach the moon.

Can you imagine the potential we all have and are not using?

There are only 3 areas of the brain you just need to know to survive in this modern world and yet so many keep using their primitive brain. Imagine having a mobile phone and not knowing how to use the apps only to answer and send txt. We have the ability to turn on or off any app in our brain. From changing moods with the switch of a lightbulb. Yes, with training you will achieve so much through these 8, S toolkit. You will be powerful, disciplined and capable to face any given situation or challenge in life.

Can you use this phone? Can you change the volume? Can you change the color?

Do you know the apps in your brain?
Can you change the noise, thoughts in your mind? Can you change your moods?

Do not turn the page this will be mind blowing.

1. The Prefrontal cortex

2. The Limbic System

3. Reptilian Brain (Brain Stem)

(So here I am thinking of all I have written in other journals that would so fit in here) all the references, all the writing and reading I did. I ran upstairs to get them out and looked, oh lord way too much, so I put them back again and here I am again. Too much knowledge is sometimes distracting. Let's make things simpler.

Take notes above on what nuggets you have got so far.

Right, let's get you introduced to your most important organ.

We have, as I said above, let's call them our 3 apps.

We will call one the Leader (Prefrontal Cortex) also called your modern brain or the CEO (behind our forehead) this is where all your decision making now and the future is made, all solutions and planning are organised.

The Protector (Brain Stem) at the base of your skull like a snake also known as the (Reptilian primitive brain). This controls all the automatics things you forget about daily. The flow of your blood etc…

The Limbic System is your emotional Brain in between both of these. Controlling all your emotions. Your short term memory lives here also. Here is where the fear and reward system exists. When this is activated in a positive way you are creative and get new ideas down on paper in a flow state. When this is activated in the system of fear, one's creativity and innovativeness is hampered. Plus resources to the other sections of the brain for example the PC/CEO stops one from making correct decisions. The name for this Fear and reward region is known as the "Amygdala". As we discussed above the limbic system is your emotional brain. I tell you the damage it causes if you cannot switch from one mood to the other.

H>A>L>T

Remember this. (I read this formula it could be Jim Kwick?)

We will all be Happy, Angry, Lonely and Tired. So, this is a normal state you are not ill. Babies just born have anxiety; they get angry for food, attached to a parent and get angry when they have to sleep.

YOU ARE NORMAL.

The last thing I will say about the limbic system is the "Amigdala" it is the controller of all the trouble in this area. It is there to protect you. The problem is people keep over activating it. (Oh, I so want to go into this but it's another book, from now you may see how obsessed I am with the workings of the brain) let's move on. Google it or maybe that is my next book.

Whooooo.... We got here. I got so carried away with the brain but it is so important that you know these 3 areas (apps) so you can live a controlled life.

To conclude the Brain app…

Listen carefully, your modern brain PFC makes decisions and motivates you to stay focused. So many successful people live from this brain and are living with a plan. The primitive brain is there to make sure we do not get into danger. For example going down a dark alley. It tells us something is not right. So many live in fear all the time of what's going to happen, fear of not taking chances, fear of going places as they live in the primitive brain awaiting for someone or something to come along like our ancestors as hunters feared being attacked and were looking over their shoulders all the time when out hunting.

I do love Shonte Jovan Taylor M.Sc a neuroscientist acquaintance of mine. Her Book "GenX" will tell you everything you need to know about the brain.

I got great advice from the book in one section with reference to your Prefrontal Cortex (behind your forehead) She says "would a painter paint over a used canvas with a painting already there?"
Why then do we constantly not clear our canvas of thoughts and start with a blank canvas for each project, decision or thought?

A great analogy.

We must know also that our brain is negatively biased. Meaning:-
It looks for the negative things first to keep us safe. Hence the anxiety and fear.

PMI, always look for the positive first, minus and then the interesting. (Coaching tool)

You need to activate your Leader brain by looking FORWARD with blinkers and not getting distracted.

Remember what function this prefrontal cortex has in helping you. Look at it when in doubt, stop living in the primitive brain, like the hunter gatherer time, out with a bow and arrow, fearing being attacked while hunting.

Look at your situation for what it actually is. Think of a solution not a problem. Do not allow your brain to get bored as it is there to help you. It is like a child also it will ramble when bored. Thinking of the past and future.

The last thing before I leave the brain section is neuroplasticity, you can make new neurons.

Just by brushing your teeth with a different hand. Going to work in a different direction. This excites the brain from being automatic in doing the same things all the time, hence it makes new neurons. What fires together wires together.

Let's get onto the main resource for a healthy brain besides food.

Sleep is the physical resource for the Brain to help it function.

When we sleep our brain is actually cleaning out chemicals. Memories are put into different files, long term memory and short term and memories we do not need. Sleep is actually like a housekeeper; it cleans out all the toxins in our brains built up while we are awake.

Regular undisturbed sleep is a necessity for every human. The animal kingdom do this. Our body and minds will never be in a healthy state without sleep. We must rest for our nervous and muscular system but most importantly our digestive system also to help absorb nutritions into our blood. Each area during the time of sleep (8 hours) gives each organ time to rest and reset. We are not machines, so many of us disrespect our bodies until it is too late. When people do this, sleep is no longer in rhythm. If a person loses the power to sleep this causes so many health problems both physical and mental.

If you look at situations of illness. This is why we have hospital beds; one is required to rest until the organ has returned to its natural state.

One tip which has gone back for centuries is to make sure your body temperature is warm. Going into a cold bed will not help the circulation and deter sleep. (This of course changed with weather and where one lives) Also your bed clothing should always be loose around your body. In the winter it is known to use a heavy blankets as a sense of security while sleeping. My dad used to put his heavy crombie coat on my bed and put a pillow down the side so I would not fall out. The weight and tucked in gives a sense of comfort. I always tucked my children in their cots and when introducing them to their new beds.

"Remember when your body moves your brain groves."

Jim Kwick.

"When your brain sleeps your body leaps"

Lillian Courtney

You are what you think, never forget this. What are you thinking now?

**4 WORDS TO DESCRIBE WHAT YOU ARE THINKING BELOW.
BE TOTALLY HONEST.**

_____

_____

_____

_____

Go into S.E.W. mode (sleep, exercise and water) add outdoor activities and having a purpose every day and you will live a focused and energised life. Lillian C.

In relation to sleep, my Dad used to work nights one week per month and he used to wake us up when he came home. I got used to sleeping late at night due to this. I remember getting up for school some mornings so tired but later in life I realised that he loved us so much, he woke us up. My mom used to get so annoyed but he loved us and missed us when working so hard.

Carrying on my late nights, I always wait until the last person in the house is in bed as I have OCD in locking up the house. I lock the doors and then wonder if I had locked them, so I will have to go and do it a few times. I wonder sometimes am I doddering but it began in childhood from my Dad at night keeping us safe as I did with my children. Do you do that?

I am way better now for going to bed early as my son Adam gave out to me, which I so appreciate as sometimes we need that someone to point out what we need to do for our health. I also am an entertainer so I would be used to late nights getting off stage and having to wind down so it takes time to de-energise and adjust your lifestyle especially after a stage show and when high dopamine is at its peak.

Before we leave the subject of sleep do you know you have your own "Chrono-type" this is your circadian rhythms. It is the levels of energy and alertness on how you achieve activities during the day.

Its meaning from the encyclopedia "Chrono" meaning relates to time and type.

You have 4 types of people. (we will discuss shortly)

If employers only went by these personality types so much more productivity would be achieved and so much more understanding of their employees.

A short true story I read whilst studying this system.

CHRONOTYPE

A lady was late every day for work. She was the best employee, best worker, they could not fault her in any way only for the fact that she was always late in the morning. They brought her into the office and discussed in detail that she was showing bad examples to the other employees and they could not give her special treatment. She discussed this with her coach looking for ideas to get her to sleep and have a routine to get up. Nothing worked. She was about to be fired but knowing she really was doing her best but her brain was active after 10am not before and late at night. (I must look into this as I come alive at night) She discussed this with her boss having been introduced to the Chronotype systems.

She asked if she could try it out for a month as she was being fired anyway so she had nothing to lose and to see how things worked out as a suggestion from her Coach. The boss agreed and to his amazement allowed her to use her chronotype. Her productivity rose even more, her health was up 70% as she was less stressed and also he was less stressed worried about what time she would turn up, which she always did but always an hour late.

I see this all the time where Leaders can see the productivity of an employee but want them to slot into their timesheet. Which is completely understandable if everyone was coming in at different times things would not work. This can be achieved if working online or a small business not in a product line obviously but different shift times for each Chronotype to suit that person would be a great way to raise productivity.

There are 4 Chronotypes:- learned during studies along the way but googled for update facts in my own words.

The Lion. The early bird up at the dawn up at 4Am sticking to routine etc…. So many fail at this level as it does not suit their chronotype.

The Early bird……. All great but are very tired early at night. It still works and so many stick with it.

The Bear

70% of people do this go to bed at 11pm and up at

7.30am (This seems to work for most people to function at a normal pace)

The Night Owl

Oh, wow I used to be and 30% still am due to
stage life and late finishing for the weekends but I do try to slot into the Bear chronotype from Mon to Friday.

Insomniacs

Insomniac people are on technology, spend their night worrying about everything. They worry about things in the past and things that might never happen.

These people stay up until mid morning am, some can function perfectly and others find it impossible to get up in the morning. When they do they will get tired during the day and very fast and go out of focus. They end up with health problem very fast in life unless they can catch a nap during the day.

I must say I am the Night owl to others as midnight going to bed and turning out the light at 1.30am or 2am is probably so late.. In the past year I have been doing my best to slot into the "Bear" for health for the future and at the suggestion of my Son Adam and I feel way more focused.

I read these details below somewhere mid my reading days but I cannot find the source. Not my information.

There are 8 material activities we hold onto:-

4 Negative and 4 positive material activities.

Negative:- Loss, shame, guilt and suffering People hold onto these and cannot let these go. Handcuffed onto these 4 above. Holding onto the shackles of life. They seem to pop up when one is just about to go to sleep.

4 Positive things we hold onto:

Positive:- Happiness, achievement, approval and fam. Why do you need approval from anyone to do anything?

Why do you need people to know what you have achieved (other than having a business and to prove your craft is credible)

Achievement yes to celebrate your children or your achievement which is amazing but do not worry about what others think, achieve things in your own time and only if you want to do them

So detach yourself from the 8 things above

Where are you at the moment?

What's your given situation at the moment?

_____

_____

All these negative and positive things cause one to be in a self prison.

To summarise:

At night saying I lost this, I am ashamed of this, I am guilty of this or worried about getting up the next morning saying "I must do this and achieve this to be approved by everyone.
Stop everything and go back to the base camp of your mind. Go back to the above chapters on the brain and learn how to use the apps we discussed. Remember you are what you think.

Life is a rollercoaster ride you have got to hold on tight and learn to face the Tsunami that have gone and are coming in your life. Look at life like a heart beat graph, the main line and the beats going up and below the line. You will have SAD times and GREAT times. Try and make life as easy as you can for yourself. Remember all humans are amess in different times of their lives.

IMAGINE NOW IN YOUR MIND THE GRAPH OF A HEARTBEAT GRAPH

YOU WILL ALWAYS HAVE UPS AND DOWNS IN LIFE.

STOP NOW and take a break.

Look up google or whatever method you have and check the heart beat diagram.

We will forever in life have ups and downs and you must be prepared to be emotionally ready to handle every given situation. Each one will be different. Look at the solutions and not the problems in all cases. Life is a B…ch and you can either cry or laugh. Learn to swim and ride the waves as you will then reach the calm seas of life.

"Life is wasted on the youth" Why because we worry about everything and analyse everything.

NOTE TAKING:-

CHAPTER 2

VALUE GRAPH

THIS IS URGENT!!!

Before we start, this is the most important question I am going to ask you.

Remember it.

I will ask you a question in the last chapter.

If you were standing on a stage and being sold in an auction for charity all your friends were there with you or colleagues. What do you think you would be sold for?

Seriously, stop reading, imagine and visualise what I have just asked you to do. The exercise below is something I will ask you about during our journey together.

EXERCISE:

Let's look at yourself value graph below:-

How much would you be sold for at a charity auction?

- 1,000 Dlrs/Euro

- 2,500 Dlrs/Euro

- 5,000 Dlrs/Euro

1,000————————————————————5,000

Put a mark on where you think you are.

What would you value yourself at? Be totally honest.
I'll repeat, What would you be sold for?" (This is fun for Charity)

Write it down and we will be looking at this at the last8th's toolkit chapter.

This number below is so important as we will look back when you have completed the 8 S toolkit.

Your Value number: …………………..

The 8's will help you through all the exercises I am going to give you.
Please do not skip them as they have worked for clients and are a proven recipe for success for your work and life.

Victor Frankl in the Nazi prison in world war 11 described his psychotherapeutic method, involving and identifying a purpose to feel positive about, then immensely imaging that outcome. The pictures you make in your head become real. Read "Man's search for meaning" you will love it

CHAPTER 3

MIND-BODY CONNECTION

2 areas in this section I want to discuss. I will not keep you long.

The conscious and subconscious mind. (Pic accredited to Marisa Peer)

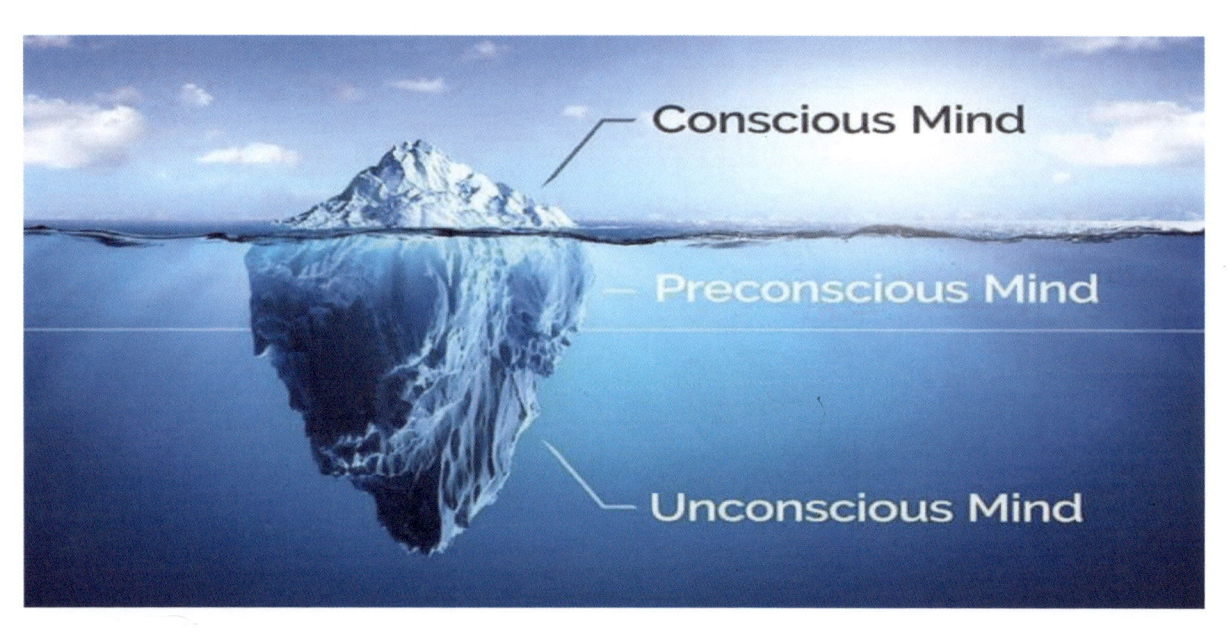

First of all, these are such **important** things you must remember and **never** forget. The subconscious mind does NOT understand any jokes.

If you say "I am stupid" you will remain that way. Yes, it is so powerful it just agrees and acts like a robot and believes. everything you tell it.

I will prove this to you now in this exercise below.

This is **so powerful** if you actually do this as **Instructed.**

THE LEMON EXERCISE:- UNIVERSAL TOOL USED BY COACHES

Right let's do this.

- Firstly, you must not have eaten or drank anything in the past 10 minutes. It will not work.

- Go to a quiet place.

Let's look at how strong your subconscious mind is.

I am trying to see what food is relevant in all countries to do this exercise.

- OK, a LEMON. I do believe everyone knows the TASTE of a lemon.

- I want you now to pretend you are sitting at a table. You have a lemon in front of you on a plate. You have a sharp knife also.

- I want you to pretend you take the knife and cut the lemon. The juice is all over your fingers.

You now cut a thin piece of the lemon and put it up to your lips. STOP, really do this please.

What can you taste?
Are you licking your lips?
Are there juices gathering in your mouth?

Is it sweet or sour?

In my lecturers 70% of people actually taste this lemon even though they have nothing in their hand.

This is so important to recognise how powerful your subconscious mind is. Imagine if you told it, you were successful or anything you want to achieve. Try it out. Remember my mistake was I thought things would happen immediately but it could actually take days, months or years.

Without action and what you tell your subconscious mind, nothing will happen.

URGENT

I know you want to get into the 8 S tool kit but this is such an amazing story you need to read it INTENTLY. All the stories you will read will be either experience from my own life and work or my client.

A TRUE STORY

THE POWER OF THE CONSCIOUS MIND
(My own personal experience)

I'll make it as short as possible.

Back in the 90's I gave birth to my Daughter Rebecca.

I was in a private hospital (I actually would now recommend a public hospital as babies are born every 15 minutes). In this private hospital maybe 8 babies per day were born. You think you are doing the correct thing. I had given birth also to my son Jonathan 18 months previous and had no complaints. I was 3 weeks overdue at this stage and was suffering from lack of sleep and had a terrible cough, plus a baby of 18 months to mind also. I had gone in and sent home as a false alarm twice.

Eventually the time came and only a slim petite nurse was there alone with another lady and myself. I asked where the gynaecologist was and she said he told her to ring him when the head was in view. At that stage I could not put up with the pressure and the pain. It was complete neglect and he arrived at the last minute 12.50am and literally I felt I was at my last gasp.

All was fine in the end and my beautiful daughter was born healthy. Thank God. We came home and after a few days I noticed the volume of my voice was going. I had no sore throat, nothing but I was lacking in volume. I must tell you I am a professional singer also and had a band at the time which so much of myincome came from. Having given up a multinational secretarial position in a top American company so as to rear my children. (I would do the exact same thing if it were now). I used to love singing to Jonathan and he knew "No place like home" at this stage and we loved singing and it was also a way of getting them to sleep. 6 days later I woke up one morning with literally no voice. It was so frightening. I am a person if you know me who just loves speaking. I suppose most Irish are storytellers.

I felt maybe it was the screaming in pain from the birth. (so different now today with so many medical aids) so I decided to let it go for a few days thinking it would come back.

Days went into weeks and things were getting worrying.

I also wanted my baby to know my voice and sing to them both.

I decided I needed professional help. I attended a vocal consultant and he sent me for tests. Nothing had been found. I attended the clinic for 12 weeks and nothing was changing, only getting worse. I was able to whisper.

I decided I needed some sort of communication and started using whistling codes (I still use today) I never thought of learning sign language which would have been the correct direction. Weeks and months went by and it was 45 Irish pounds every week for the consultant. That probably around 70 or 80 euro now.

The consultant advised me that I should speak to another colleague of his as he was baffled also as to why I could not speak.

I was at home and the phone rang. I could not reply but picked it up and whistled into it so as to let the person know that I was there (in case it were friends or family) She immediately started introducing herself.
I at that stage had a slight whisper and I remember her words. "Whatever you do, do not whisper". She asked to see me at her office and I was at the end of my theader with no results that I was so happy to have someone interested in my case.

As a strong-minded person. I tried everything to speak. Why could I not, What was the problem?

"The morning came when I had to meet my new consultant." Patricia Cullin.

We discussed my situation. I could not speak but I could get communication out with a slight whisper.
She encouraged me and said she would have me back speaking.

We worked together for a few months. It came to my attention that when I went into her office I could say a few words but when I left her office I could not speak again.
This was getting very frustrating.
Eventually we reached a stage where I could speak but had rules on what to do.

This is where it gets really interesting.

Getting back to my band in the 80's and 90's we had a great name in the city and outside. We were booked a year to 2 years in advance. So, rewinding before I lost my voice we had been hired for a New Years eve party in one of the prominent hotels outside the town.
I immediately rang them and it was in May of that year so there was plenty of notice that I would have a stand in. I was going by orders from my vocal consultant.

The night arrived it was December 31st and my consultant told me I could try one song but no way a full night. Things were so exciting my voice, well only, at her office was coming back (still not ok outside her office). No one could understand.

The band set up, people started to arrive and the place was packed to the doors. I told the band and my stand-in that I would stay at the private bar outside for a while so people could get used to the situation.

That is when all hell broke loose (as we say in Ireland, but this is just a figure of speech, not literally).

The Manager came into the bar after me and asked why I was not getting ready to go on stage. I explained to him what had happened and that in May of that year I had sent an email and confirmed everything and they had agreed.

His words will stay in my mind forever. He said "you have 2 choices. Do not sing and I will sue you or do not sing and you can pay every person in the hall back their money".

Where would I get that money and I literally was in such a state. Also stress would literally take away any voice. I had worked so hard for where I had come and I knew if I sang I might never be able to speak to my children and sing to them again.

I ran into the band guys and told them the situation. They said no way as they felt I would ruin the night with no voice. I said look I am allowed one song and when I singpeople will know my situation.

The drummer was in a state, the bass player confused as to what the hell we would do and my husband who was the guitar player ran to the bathroom in shock.

I said let's do this. I was literally devastated but knew I had to sing. The place was packed. One song was allowed by Patricia. The drummer started the intro, the lads just stared at me and the Manager was at the end of the hall with folded arms in an aggressive stance.

Would anything come out? Omg what will I do? What a situation?

Lead guitar, bass and drums and it was my turn to start. My stand -in was ready in case anything happened.

The combined stress was cutting like a knife on stage. My stand-in just looked on the ground and I felt I could just stay on the stage if all came to it. I started the song. At this stage I could barely speak and had not tried to sing before this but I had been told I could by my consultant.

I started to sing and I can only tell you I sang with a hoarse voice but to my surprise and amazement I sang and I am singing from that moment up to now.

What the hell had happened? To this day I will never understand the power of my subconscious mind.

I had got a fright giving birth and my subconscious mind shut down in that area. I had tried everything. Medics had tried everything. Patricia Cullin had succeeded in getting me so far.

A fright put me into a situation and brought that area back.

Please listen to me. I am a very strong-minded person and nothing could get my voice back.

What else is your subconscious mind stopping you from doing?

At one of the festivals back singing after the event.

IT IS SO POWERFUL.

Is there anything that you used to do to perfection and now cannot do? Maybe something happened to you in that area?

This is just one story I will put in here to give you my experience on my journey.

CHAPTER 4

4 INTELLIGENCES

Before we begin our 8's toolkit I want you to realise that we have 4 intelligences which so many do not even realise. Notes taken while studying The 7 habits of successful people by Steven Covey's. He believed we had 4 areas I will just mention 3.

I am not going to go into these but I do want you to google and get to know each one.

We have our IQ, Our Mind (Mental Intelligence)

PQ...................... Our Body (Physical Intelligence)
EQ......................Our Heart (Emotional Intelligence)
SQ...................... Our Spirit (Spiritual Intelligence)

If you can keep all above healthy you will live in a very peaceful and controlled state. Scientific studies have proven the close relationship between the body, mind and heart.

Physical thinking and feeling.

Mind- Body connection is of such great interest to you if you really delve into it.

Even the philosophers Descartes and Hume discussed in the book "Philosophy made simple" by Richard H Popkin PH.D and Avrum Stroll PH.D, both philosophers spent their time discussing the mind and body, to see if they were connected to the other.

I believe that everything that happens in your life, your thoughts and actions affect the mental and physical body and vice versa. Happiness is not an outer condition it is an inner. Control of thoughts.

Shakespeare said "Nothing is good or bad but thinking makes it so"

Lincoln said "Most people are as happy as they make their minds up to be"

Everyone is aiming for the same thing in life and that is happiness, love, peace of mind, health and financial stability. Put 2 people in the same situation and they will have 2 completely different experiences. That is because of thought control.

Social media I must state now that I think it is such an amazing invention.

Scrolling on social media in certain circumstances is extremely dangerous for the mind. Looking at disturbing events that come up, cyber bullying affects this new generation. By looking at other's lives who pretend to be living this way or actually are, causes the scroller to desire and envy what they are looking at in some cases. So many times nothing is REAL.

You see children being brought to drs now with depression.

I overheard a friend saying her son had no energy, was putting on weight and suffering from terrible headaches. The Dr told her to take away her son's digital equipment during certain times during the day and to get him outdoors and to add activities.

What is fantastic are Games, which to me are educational and help the mind to think, make out rules and open up creativity for the user. I do believe they should be time boxed.

Constant scrolling and using the www other than for information, work or knowledge can cause so much physical and mental illness that did not exist in previous generations.

Your actions affect your mind, your thoughts affect your body and your feelings.

Jim kwik in his book "Limitless" he gave 4 outstanding explanations of social media overload. (Remember I am just talking about people on it all the time and others who scroll endlessly, I believe Social media is outstanding and the www is a great way for people to keep in contact especially for work and life).

These 3 points below are from his book "Limitless" which I really think are of great relevance to everyone's life.

1. Digital Deluge:- Compared to the 15 Century we now consume as much data in a single day as an average person from the 1400s would consume in an entire lifetime. Now we have so much access to information it is affecting our time and quality of life.

2. Digital Distraction:- People are always on, ever connected all the time and distracted and are struggling to stay focused with family and work. People have a fear of missing out (FOMO) if not online. A study of 300 students showed those who had their phones with them and those who had put them away had completely different experiences. Ryan Dwyer of University of British Columbia's research showed the student who left their phones off enjoyed a meal and were more focused. While the other students were looking at their phones and wanted to reply plus could not enjoy the meal thinking about what they were missing.

3. Ryan Dwyer stated "modern technology may be wonderful, it can easily sidetrack us and take away from the special moments we have with family and friends in person".

4. Digital Dementia

We are not giving our brains a chance to work naturally. Hence, we are getting very forgetful.

Be the security guard at all times to the gate of your mind.

PART 2

CHAPTER 5

THE BEGINNING OF OUR 8'S TOOLKIT

A person who takes control of his actions always finds away out. The envy of others must show you that you are worth something.

Let us take a rest and start our journey through the most powerful tools that will help you in all areas of your life.

If you have read as far as here and have not skipped to our 8 S toolkit I am so proud of you. Remember, I told you this could end up a pocket book or something else as I go along. Bear with me on this new journey of such excitement and I hope you are enjoying it as much as I am. I literally cannot wait to get back home each night to chat to you all.

So, let's look at Emotional Intelligence through 8 of my S'tool kits and what it really is. Why we were not made aware of this tool kit in school?

Take for example; we all have been introduced to IQ… Our level of intelligence.
What about our EI (Our Emotional Intelligence)?
My explanation is to be aware of how you CONTROL your EMOTIONS in any given situation.

8.1

1. Self-Awareness-Awareness of your own emotions

It is a necessity in these uncertain times to be awake. I see a huge shift in history and I feel that a lot of people are unprepared to manage themselves, be it on a life or work emotional level.

I want you to awaken your creative ideas which are so important at the moment with the shift in history.

How aware are you of what is actually happening around you and also to you?
You will often hear people say "If I had known at the time I would have done differently"

Who are you really?

The following exercise will help you find out very quickly. This is a coaching exercise from my Dip in Business & Personal coaching from the ILI

Title the exercise:

I AM ……………

I wrote this:-

I am a mother, wife, professional singer, honest, confident person, confidence coach, reliable, hard worker, genuine, poet, writer, adviser, musician and spiritual being

Now make your list.

You can complete in pencil or do on a separate page.

I AM.
……………………………..

_____

_____

_____

_____

Now priorities each one starting at No 1 as being the top number.

Most of my clients make a list and then priorities in a different format unless they feel strongly about something.

Your next exercise:-

Title the Exercise

He/She is:-

Write a list of all the things you think people think of you.
Who do people think you really are?

_____

_____

_____

_____

Now priorities each one from 1 upwards as being the top.

Why this exercise? One of my clients was really confident but could not show that outside.
Promotions, anything to do with confidence they were not added in any activity. This hampered all their opportunities in work and life until we did this exercise. We looked and saw that on the He/She section (what others thought of him) it said "shy and timid". To him he was confident and assertive.

We need to project **WHO WE ARE.**

After a few coaching sessions he used his talents to the full and changed his perception of how he projected himself.

Another client really thought they were not liked and when they handed around the form I had given them people said they were friendly, happy and helpful.

Never take things personal and project who you really are with confidence, be self aware of how you are in the present moment with others.

We all have different versions of ourselves in work, home and social situations. You being authentic in each area as these are your characters to fit into society. I am my true self all the time but obviously I have a professional self for work and a chill self for home. We all have a "Social self" **and "an** Essential Self.

Above exercise gives you an idea of how you feel about yourself and how you are projecting your honest true self.
Be careful also who you give the "He is/she is" form. Make sure they have nothing against you as they will then perceive the incorrect information for you, projecting their solo perception of you. Get a few people who know you well to do the exercise also and listen now to me take nothing personal.
You are who you believe you are.

Most people said I was kind, confident and a great mother, singer and coach. Others said I was snobby and wanted leadership too much until we spoke after for the first time and we laugh now at it. In saying that, did I give this impression without knowing it?

Perception is strange.

As we may not realise what others think of us.

We can hurt people along the way also without even realising it as maybe we may be going through things ourselves at the time. Check your list of family and friends and see how you have been with them.

Kindness and love is so important and it will follow you all your life if you give it out.

"Surely goodness and kindness shall follow you all the days of your life".

BE YOU. There is no perfect person; we are only learning ourselves as we grow.

I also remember a guy coming to paint my house and said after 17 years coming to paint my house how I was so kind and so many said not to work for me as I was a snob. You have to live with someone to know them. You have to walk in someone's shoes t.o know what they are going through before making any opinions.

To me my authentic self is happy, confident, a genuinely caring mother, a spiritual being in a human body as I connect everyday with my inner being and feed that daily with light, breath and prayer which to me is the same as meditation.
Faith keeps me on the right road.

Please read the book "The 4 Agreements". By Don Miguel Ruiz

2 main points I took from his book that really helped me in life were:-

1. TAKE NOTHING PERSONAL

2. SEEK FIRST TO UNDERSTAND.

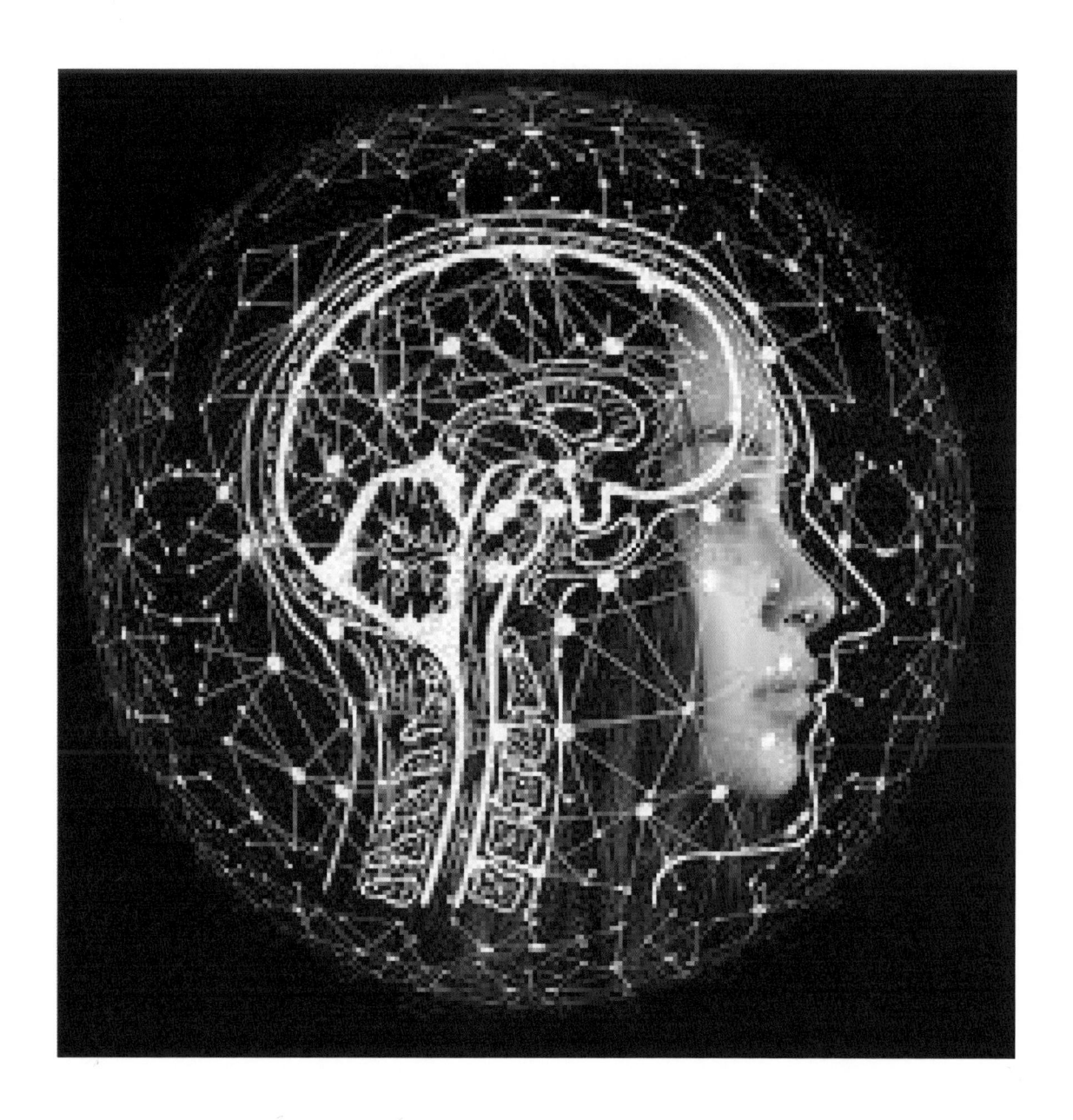

CHAPTER 6

HOW TO FIND YOUR TRUE SELF (SELF AWAKENESS)

8.2

I do not know what you got out of the above exercise but it was urgent that you see and become aware of who you really are. The true authentic self. Under all the layers of the onion of life we will peel them off and find you. The confident, strong self before paradigms and life took over.

How about that? Let's get this sorted once and for all.

The HELICOPTER exercise. This will blow your mind. (Coaching tool)

I need you to read the instructions before you do this exercise.
When finished I want you to follow the instructions as I have written down.

HELICOPTERING UP (look at your real self)

Sit comfortably with your feet flat on the ground. Make sure you have no distractions. I want you to close your eyes, relax and drop your shoulders. Take a deep breath, 4 in and hold and slowly exhale. Do this 2 times.

What is the person up there like? What is the person down here like? Find YOU. The authentic self is up there, bring it down to join your earthly self.

Diagram Self recognition

Now I want you to imagine yourself above yourself. I now want you to look up at you and take note of what is different with the person up there and you down here? (Concentrate take note of everything you see)

How do you look? What are you wearing? What way are you standing or sitting?
How are you acting? Shy or confident?
Relax and take in everything. Remain silent.

Now I want you to rise up into that person and look down at you here from above.
Look at you down here.
What is the difference?
What do you need to change?
Now **"THIS IS URGENT"**

I need you to come BACK DOWN into yourself (this is urgent) and OPEN your eyes.

How was that?

If you did this exercise correctly you will have found amazing information about yourself. The person up there is your true authentic self whereas the person down here is drenched with paradigms from parents, school, siblings, jobs, relationships etc....

(Take note that a lot of people may have reached this already and not see any difference so congratulations) When I was training as a coach we did this exercise. I saw (myself) with long brown hair floating above me and I had cut my hair at the time. She was slimmer and just seemed to flow with the most beautiful white dress and elegance. It was me but the confident, assertive real me. I decided there and then I was going to become or return to that person. I kept a picture in my mind and worked on it every day after that and I realised one day after months I was morphing into her. I had changed the colour of my hair and let my hair grow.

It was actually about 5 year and one day I looked into the mirror and just realised I had returned to whom I so longed to be for such a long time. The me I had been brought up to be. The me, I felt inside but was taken away by paradigms and beliefs and ways of others and the ropes of life and work. Like everyone in life goes through. You will find yourself.

Keep the image of that person
you saw in your mind. It is the best version of yourself.
**Every day see this person, become this person as this is
really you**

Did you write down all the things you really are?

How amazing you are?

I bet you feel a sense of SELF? (If you did this exercise correctly you will have achieved so much in these last few chapters). If you feel it did not work please go back again and concentrate and accept and allow it to happen.

I do this exercise once a month to keep myself in line.

Assert yourself to take action on all above so far.

Before we leave self awakeness and self awareness I believe the 4th missing leg of the square of power money and fame has finally seeped into the world. Wisdom or gratitude. Like a chair without this leg you will not be balanced in work and life. To those who grew up with this instilled seem to handle these uncertain times in a more positive and healthy way. Others have also reset in these uncertain times.

1. Take nothing personal
2. Seek first to understand
3. Do your best, everyone's best is different. (3 points from "The 4 Agreements" book)

It is never too late to RESET, RECHARGE AND REGAIN your STRENGTH and INNER BEING. Lillian C.

CHAPTER 7

SELF-BELIEF

8.3

Think about this statement. Just stop for a minute. Do you believe in yourself? Really think this one out. Are you following your vision, your goals and listening to you, not what others believe in you.

We were born with the full potential equipped with the software (our Brain) to accomplish anything we put our minds to.

What do you believe about yourself? What you can achieve etc..
I want you now to make out a work Performance profile (if in that situation)

A Self-assessment Profile
A job analysis profile
A Personal Development Profile

What do you believe you can achieve in all above?

_____

What is your action plan?

_____

What will you do?

_____

1 to 10 which one above is important or stood out to you?

I want you now to go and get some exercise, take a break or just get a drink. If in bed reading this relaxes and chills.

I'm going to show you a graph which came into my mind from so many clients, the way they looked at themselves. I called it the self cage belief system.

Check out my diagram below. Please spend time to understand it.

The "1" and the "Me" when not in sync nothing will every work out in life. You being the worst bully to yourself means you have nowhere to escape to.

1. You calling yourself to listen, You saying negatives things to you.
2. You sitting up to call you, you listening to others and not yourself still speaking negatively to yourself.
3. You eventually standing up to yourself not accepting you to lower your standards or yourself value for others and yourself.
4. You finally accepting yourself, loving yourself and finally becoming the "WE"

Learn to love and value yourself by the practice of listening to yourself

When you become the **1 + Me = WE** you have a home inside yourself to come home to. A place you can chat to yourself and not find fault.
Check out the diagram now and really look over it.

I want you now to sit down and stay still.

Find somewhere really comfortable. I want you to close your eyes take a good deep breath, hold and let it out slowly.
Imagine a light coming from above your head beaming right down into your inner being to the pit of your stomach. I want you to think of your stomach area or heart area as a beautiful room. Make it out as you want, design it, what colour is it. Make it your safe place to come home to when out of peace of mind. A happy place. Now allow the light come into that space and go around and clean everything in all areas. Any darkness let there be light.
This is such a great exercise as no matter what situation you have a lovely home safe to some back into your mind, instead of a mixed up jumbled worrying space.

You must say

We will be fine, We are ……………………………

The "I" always seems to dominate the "ME" therefore always from now on respect and value you and apologise to yourself if you speak badly to yourself.

How to find out if you are doing this to yourself. Answer this question.

Would you speak to me the way you speak to yourself? Yes/No

Most would say no way. Why?

There's the answer on how you are treating yourself.

MY STORY: 1

A little story I want you to chill and read. Go and get a cup. **A true story** that happened to me and it changed my direction in life from my vision but also I blamed the person for it for years.

I was 12 years of age when Sr Kate the Nun teaching me in my convent school brought me down to play the church organ. This was like a dream come true for me. I had visualised it for years even wrote an essay about it. Years passed and I had been playing for years until I was 18 or 19 years of age. Sometimes I would cover a wedding or mass later.

It was a beautiful Sunday morning and I was playing for 11am mass. Someone had used the organ before me that morning and I had not even realised it until I sat into the organ bench. I normally used the pull out button system from the top of the organ not the pedals but to my horror the pedals were on. I could not turn them off, also every time I put my feet down a terrible sound roared around the church. Think about this the organ had been taken from the balcony to the top of the church by the alter so everyone could see who was playing. I could not get out from the bench as I had sat in too far and it was too distracting to achieve during mass.

In my mind I kept saying everyone will be laughing at me, the embarrassment. (If it were now I would just laugh it off) being vulnerable and at the teenager stage, this was huge to me. I finally completed the task of finishing the mass and when I got to the end of the church a guy came over and said. "OMG you were a laughing stock everyone was laughing at you that was terrible." I'd never go back again if I were you"

What did I do?

I listened to his words they kept ringing in my ear. "You were a laughing stock" Because I also believed this to be true I started to water the seed of Self belief leading to Self doubt in my ability to do what I loved and I was so brilliant at doing. I had been brought up to Professor Fleishman and given the opportunity to study at

UCC (University college Cork) so many great opportunities but this seed was getting stronger every day.

I left the church playing the organ and never returned. Every time I played the piano when no one was around I was just in the flow state without a mistake and when anyone came along I just lost track of my fingers. For years this was going on. Until one day I realised it was not the person's fault it was the belief I had in myself to continue. I allowed this person to take the controls of the steering wheel of my life and direct it off my path. It was **MY FAULT.**

Having that realisation changed my whole life. I began playing my instruments again. Composing wonderful music and enjoying my new found realisation of self belief.

How I loved my music. Playing the organ in the church from 12, until I was 19 years of age. Lack of self belief can change the direction of your whole life.

A CLIENT'S EXPERIENCE OF LACK OF SELF BELIEF

I got a call from a friend whose daughter was going for an interview for a job she had tried to get for 5 years. She had all the qualifications and people who came into the job after her were getting promoted to similar positions. She had wanted this position for 5 years. The interview was the following day at 2.30pm so we made an urgent appointment. I said I would do my best to see how I could help her through a Self belief toolkit.

We went over everything. Why she felt she did not get it 2 years in a row.

We went over her CV and experiences.

I noticed a few months were missing having come from working abroad on her **CV** and she said she had been working in a company doing the exact same service as the one she was going for but did not put it down. This was the golden ticket. She had the experience and was afraid to put it down in case they felt she might leave them also.

No 1: I suggested she retype the cv and enter this golden nugget.

No 2: When doing the mock interview her posture, and projection of speech was not confident projecting her belief in her ability to take up the position.

We stayed at this for about 2 hours and I told her to go home and stand in front of the mirror and keep practicing her elevator pitch and every time she did she was to say "I have the job. I am a............................."

We discussed every aspect. She was worried in case she came across too cocky and arrogant but the job was a very important position of leadership in one of the large corporations. If you are leading a team you must believe in yourself so that the team can believe that you can lead with authority.

She came to me an hour before the interview the next day.

We practiced the mock interview putting highlight on the experience shehad working in a large position in London to bring all she had learned with her also to help the team.

2:30 pm, I looked at the clock. 3:30pm, No call.

What was happening? I was as nervous as she had been for her.

We had not discussed if she did not get the position as I said we could wait until she got the results. Why worry over a worry that might not happen.

I was with a client when the phone rang. She was crying and could not speak.
I had told the client I was waiting for an urgent call.

Having calmed down she told me the wonderful news, she had got the position and it was all due to her having experience and having travelled and worked in the said area and new belief and value in here skills.

THE MORAL OF THE STORY:

Use all your toolkit, talents and experiences and believe you can do it. The energy and injection of success for my client gives me this happiness inside to see them come alive with such new found self belief.

I could give you so many stories from client opening successful business having come to me with nothing. Lacking in energy from trying to think of the future to now CEO's of their own companies.

All lacking Self Belief that they could take each challenge.

I recommend the book "Screw it, let's do it "by Richard Branson. Having read this book I took some chances in business and succeeded. My stories would be way too long, maybe the next book :)

CHAPTER 8

SELF-CONFIDENCE

8.4

Confidence what does it mean? To confide in oneself.

Confidence cannot be taught overnight. It is a skill. It has to be built up over time with practice.

There are so many different categories in confidence.

Social confidence, self-confidence, group confidence and situational confidence that we all have to face. One must be prepared for the new world ahead with this new found powerful confidence.

I want you to think of a person with confidence. What do they walk like, wear clothes like. speak like, express energy like? Think about someone walking into a room. Head up shoulders back stomach in and chest out. Really, think of someone you know with confidence. Of course, they do not come in with bent shoulders crunched down and speaking low. Would you have confidence in that type of person to advise you or the energetic person well dressed and confident in speech?

Confidence should be worn like a coat. You must build it up like a muscle. If you go to the gym you do not walk out after 1 or 2 night with muscles, you must practice and build that muscle of confidence.

This was my very first workshop. I did not know how it would go. I was awake walking around thinking, am I an imposter? (Imposter Syndrome) this happens to most people beginning a business. It was the most energising day of my life. I realised how beneficial Business and Life Coaching was needed in all areas and most importantly, I did not need to know anything about any area other than my own, what I was teaching. That was my fear.

Do you know as a child and early teenager I had no Self confidence. Yes, on stage, I came alive but once off the stage I was a frightened deer. At 7 how did I know I could transfer my personality with my conscious mind?

For those who suffer, yes, I say suffer as I really believe lack of confidence causes anxiety if not checked early on in life. You need to allow children to take chances, fall off bikes and trees, make decisions and become self leaders to head out it to this jungle of a world. Confidence in people, anxiety and so many more issues can be healed and sorted.

Everything has to do with practice, rinse and repeat. Getting out in society, joining groups, teams, speech, one's posture and socialising can be affected by lack of confidence. Jobs, promotions, relationships and so much more are affected.

Looking back through the last year of clients they have the capability, talents, accreditations, have worked in the area and have huge portfolios. Yes so many had not the motivation as they get this block and do not have the confidence to get up and go.

I wrote a few tips here for you:

1. Being realistic, fake it till you make it is fine but to me you MUST have the TOOLS to prove your knowledge.

2. Confidence is not arrogance, Don't be arrogant, it's wearing the coat of confidence, don't ever feel superior to others or make them feel that way, it's not confidence.

3. Confidence is the knowledge to know in yourself to know you can achieve and do what you have set out to do. Belief brings confidence.

Confidence is the PETROL

Confidence is the muscle that you build up gradually, it does not just happen.

CONFIDENCE is your thought pattern.

We are not trained about our fight and flight pattern. What frightens us?

(Modern brain and primitive brain) Go back to the Brain chapter. Google "Amygdala" (this is another area I give workshops on)

Confidence is the ability to belief in yourself and 100% have certainty in the benefits it will have for other people.

Imagine the Power you would have for your team or yourself if you could build this amazing confidence.

Write down what talent you have that you can use at this moment, be it work or creativity.

EXERCISE:

TALENT SEARCH

I want you now to get a pen and notebook and write down what you feel you are capable of doing. What talents you have that you could make a living out of now or even a hobby (that could lead to a living in so many cases) or just for pleasure and relaxation.

Remember when you're going to make a presentation or going out in life it takes 90 days to build a habit. Wear your coat of confidence until you build that confidence inside you.

A confident person walks the walk and talks the talk. Stand straight, speak confidently and get your ideas and visions out to the world.

TIPS ON HOW TO BUILD CONFIDENCE

- I strongly suggest you practice confidence.

- Look at the person you want to be and start acting like that person. It will take time but you will get there. Make sure you do not build arrogance but confident.

- Confidence is an air of authority and self awareness, arrogance is egotism, self importance over others.

- Posture is everything. Stand tall and dress with style.

- Use clear language when speaking and use a confident tone

- Make eye contact with whom you are in company with.

- Practice positive self-talk

- Always have a daily, weekly and monthly purpose and set achievable goals and work towards them

- Learn from your mistakes and failures

- Celebrate your accomplishments, no matter how small

- Surround yourself with positive and supportive people

- Face your fears and take on new challenges and step outside of your comfort zone

- Focus on your strengths and talents not your weaknesses

- Exercise regularly

- Avoid comparing yourself to others

- Take care of your mental and physical health

Remember that confidence takes time to build, so be patient with Yourself.

I believe every child should be sent to drama and stage classes. This changed my life in every way.

TRUE LIFE EXPERIENCE

Before we leave this section I want you to sit back go and get a coffee, tea, beer, wine or water and settle in to another one of my true life experiences on confidence.

I was very shy as I had already told you, rewind back to 14 years of age and you know I came alive on stage but off it I was like a frightened deer. My mother was always playing the piano and singing all the great show songs of her era. Hence standing on the couch with a hair brush I always had a vision of myself in the Opera House.

One day I came in from school and she had an advert from the local paper saying there was a theatrical group looking for members. She had cut it out and I rang and an audition was organised. To cut a long story short I got the audition and spent 5 years in the Opera House and going to festivals with the group called "the Penny Youth Theatre. I just loved it and after all these years rejoined only 2 years ago again.

Well to continue my story at 19, I left for London to visit my sister who lived there with her children and husband. I was only going over for a week but on leaving she begged me to stay. I had no intentions of and my flight was at 4pm that day. She worked in the Samual and Montague Bank at the time and I went in early with her to London to shop and chill before leaving. On walking around as my luggage was in the bank, I saw an advertisement in a recruitment window.

Looking for a "confident bubbly person" for a large company. I had no intention of taking the job but I decided just to get the experience of what London was like so I called in. If I did want the job I probably would have been in a state. I went into the office and the lady gave me a card with an address. The London Metal Exchange, Grace church St at 12 noon. It was only 10.30am so I had no suitable clothes. I went to the bank to my sister and we swapped ends, I borrowed her skirt, actually the bank uniform.

Her colleagues laughed as they said they always wanted the job there and I had no intention of getting it. I walked into the interview. It was a huge glass skyscraper and something like a series on TV. Large plants, beautiful people all dressed in amazing suits. If I was going for the interview really I would have ran out the door. I sat waiting and Richard Wells called me into his office. I automatically decided I would go into character as I had been trained as an actress. "I am now a top secretary and contract dealer of Gold and Iron Ore in the Stock exchange'. I went into character. My stance changed, I walked tall, totally confident and sat in front of his desk.

My father said when you shake someone's hand squeeze so tight they feel your heart (which I did and believe to this day I got the job over it). He started coughing and I ran out the door looking for water and brought it back in and handed him a tissue from my bag (Which I only had as I had to put my makeup on in the bank). He asked if I could wait and he left me there for about 10 to 15 Mins. The view all over London was just breath taking coming from Cork and where I lived. He returned and offered me the job and to start the following day. I literally did not know where to look. I nearly left my theatrical role that I was playing as if on stage.

We parted and I ran to the bank to my sister. What would I do? What an opportunity. The wages were insane, my own office, training and an apartment in London. What would I do, this had all been an act. I did not know where to turn, go or stay? My self confidence was nowhere near the person I had been in the interview and now I had to be me if I took it. Shy but very efficient. Fake it till you make it. I had the tools and the education so what was going to stop me. Lack of confidence. These people were way ahead of me, it was a place I felt I did not belong, would I be able? Self doubt like never before and once again like the organ in the church seeped up to the very essence of my being.

Theatre had helped me so much but this was a different level.

I had left my music over that guy other than theatre and singing with the group, would I allow this lack of confidence stop me from taking this job?
I decided with the persuasion of my sister to stay and take it.

I loved every minute.

What stopped you or is stopping you from taking opportunities like this?

CHAPTER 9

SELF CONTROL

8.5

Some points may be longer than others just stay with me as I am passionate to give you as much information and coaching tools in this book to help you evolve as a great leader in your work and life areas. Plus a great life balance and peace of mind.

Self and Control: What do these 2 words mean to you?

To me it is to be in control of your emotions that will lead to you being in control of every part of your life. As your emotions affect every decision you make, every action in both your work and life areas.

I ask my students and clients this question.

If you were in a taxi would the driver give you the controls of the steering wheel?

Yes or No?

Why not? Write your answer down below no matter what it is. This will really bring to light the actions of control of YOUR LIFE.

Why then do we as humans allow people to take control of our thoughts, decisions and lives? Yes so many of us have allowed people to do that without consciously even realising it. Maybe until it is too late.

As children we probably were the leader or follower with friends. We might not have wanted to go to something as simple as an event but followed.

As a teenager we asked friends or siblings if this dress or suit was nice or not.? Simple examples like this will show you how a person will be in work and life. Never ever allow anyone to control your life.

People have great ideas and ask others for advice and get their ideas diluted in their mind.

When people get married there are 2 people in the marriage, you will see one person morph into the others personality. It's all about that person.

Marriages should be that each person has their own Friends, their own hobby. Plus then their own time together.

Think of your life as that steering wheel.

Never allow anyone else's hand on your steering wheel; you're the driver of your own life.

Has someone your steering wheel?

Be strong make changes if you need to and hold on TIGHT. Make your own decisions. Never allow anyone to dampen your vision.

EXERCISE FOR SELF CONTROL

An exercise which the coaching industry use. It's NOT mine.

This is so powerful it can be used for any given situation. Used by the FBI, government agencies and top companies and agencies also.

This is a very important Exercise if you practice this it will help you control any emotion and give you your power back also keep you calm in any given situation to make a decision with a clear and focused mind.

I would like to take the credit for this exercise but it is a coaching exercise I gained from my Business & Personal Coaching class at ILI

S + R = E

Stimulus + Reaction = Eventual Outcome

Stimulus:-

Something that makes you happy, sad or angry. Something triggers those emotions above.

Reactions:-

How you immediately react when anything triggers you.

Eventual Outcome:-

What action or emotions come out of the reaction or the eventual outcome of the action you take to the stimulus above?

I want to give you the **GREATEST GIFT** that so many do not realise exists in all of us. This will raise your Emotional Intelligence to a higher level knowing this.

It is the gift of "SELF CONTROL" using these 3 keys but the one gift below I am going to relate to you will blow your mind.

I will now give you the key to unlock the door to this part of your mind and SELF CONTROL.

Between Stimulus and Reaction you have another action. Yes we all have it but we do not use this golden gift.

It is the "RESPONSE"

Think about it.

Imagine if something annoyed you and you reacted with stress and anger what do you think the eventual outcome would be?

You will either strike out verbally or sometimes people react physically.

You will, like most people, get into a state, your heart beating fast, angry and your emotions will be all over the place. Your energy will be depleted. Your focus will be disrupted. The effect on the outcome of the actions to the other person or thing will be on our mind. It could be a job, a friend or family situation.

Let's turn this around with the gift of "Response" time.

Let's take the scenario again.

NEW STORY of the same experience.

Someone annoyed you. You change from reaction to response thinking. Give yourself time to respond. Think of the outcome before responding.

If I react with angry .... Outcome.........Stress

If I react with response thinking– Outcome— Calm discussion.

If I use response thinking outcome, the communication level and conversation will be discussed calmly and if not, yes it will on your side of the discussion.

Yes, you can get your point across by calmly speaking. Look at the difference.

Dealing with an angry boss or difficult person this is the greatest gift.

I constantly repeat in my mind "SRE, SRE, SRE" if someone or something is annoying me, it really has helped me in life and work.

Please do this exercise, write it down and get to know the formula.

Say after me, SRE, SRE, use this and get into the habit of using it by saying it while walking around and look at it daily and see how you can use this. It can be used for any given situation.

This is a coaching tool exercise.

Try it out.

TIPS ON SELF CONTROL

Your day should start the night before.

Before you do anything after getting out of bed, make it, before you start your day. This will give you a clean start to the day and a comfortable place to get into at night helping your sleep

- Use my coaching tools in each "S" tool throughout the book. Identify your triggers (SRE) and know when and why you tend to lose self-discipline and control
- Have a clear vision to set clear and specific goals for yourself.

- Practice mindfulness and meditation to increase self-awareness and reduce stress to gain a disciplined persona in work or life
- Change anything negative into a positive thought. Use PMI, "Positive, Minus an Interesting" to dilute and dissect any situation. Affirmations to boost your confidence, motivation and energy.
- Develop a support network of friends or family who can help you stay accountable and motivated.
- Use visualisation and mental rehearsal to prepare for challenging situations.
- Create a plan of action for how you will handle difficult situations when they arise.

- Practice self-care and prioritise your physical and emotional needs.
- Celebrate your successes and acknowledge your progress along the way.
- Remember that self-control is a skill that can be developed and improved with practice and patience.

CHAPTER 10

SELF-DISCIPLINE

8.6

Tips on Self Discipline

What does this mean to you?

To me it is to be able to achieve and stick with a goal or project consistently until you have it done. To stick with what you have said you will do and to have the discipline to see it through.

Example:-

I have the discipline to stay on my health diet every week and allow one day per week to rest.

It is so hard to be disciplined by the people around you, who are putting temptation your way. Lillian Courtney

It is better to be alone than to be with disruptive people taking you off track

Lillian Courtney

NOTES:

Here are some tips on self-discipline:

- Make out a plan and goal and stick to it.

- Make out a vision board to track your progress.

- Remove distractions and temptations.

- Become self-confident to stick to your plan through self-awareness.
- Surround yourself with supportive people.

- Keep reminding yourself of the benefits.

- Decide on a completion date. Add that extra time to give yourself a finish line.

REWARD YOURSELF EVERY STEP OF THE WAY AT EACH CORNER.

I want to discuss an example of Self Discipline to you from one of my client's point of view.

I get so many clients coming in with lack of motivation, lack of confidence, lack of focus, lost in a fog at a crossroads. relationship problems, career direction and business ideas.

These are just a few of the one-to-one Personal Development clients I coach. In Business I also coach in the area of team training whereby time management due to lack of discipline in keeping with the finish deadline has been a problem.

A top Corporate Manager came to me with this issue: Lack of Self Discipline. He was confident, looked great and spoke with a professional tone. He walked into my office and I really felt he had the wrong door.

He had a strong posture and clear friendly smile. I had seen it all before but this was a tricky one. He so looked all together.

He had great ideas for the company he worked for but he had no discipline whatsoever, having told me his situation.

He was not, first of all, consistent with anything he started, but had been in the company for over 8 years. They introduced everything into a digital format. This is where everything went wrong. He had been offered a chance to take over a good position in the company. He had the qualifications but had not the discipline to get the work completed on time and nothing seemed to have been working. It was his last chance (he quoted) as he was about to be fired. Hence, he hired me urgently to help him out.

I felt a stubborn attitude was his problem.

We worked through this together for 4 weeks. In the first week he was all go and finally he slipped into this mood of "could not be bothered" pattern. He was learning new systems but the company wanted him to get faster at the software. Now if you know me or have been to one of my coaching sessions the first thing I will tell you is that I mean business. My reputation is on the line if I do not succeed in changing what is bothering you. I have OCD with my work, it is so important and I am passionate as I have seen the results in others who have gone through my program.

I will tell you immediately that I am boot camp, I will push you to the limit and if I do not see a response back I will discuss it once, if that doesn't work I will call you up on it and the 3rd time I will have to flag you. Once the client knows this they will understand the system I work through.

The system I work through is, I ask and dig to see what is CAUSING this situation? How can we go forward and fix it not looking at the problem ever but the solution once I know the situation.

I have a toolkit of powerful coaching tools. So many I have designed from different client experiences and how I handled that situation. We always find out if it's bad habits, be it time management, late nights, no routine, the wrong perception of the situation, could be health, relationship, in the wrong place, not their vision, so many issues and many more. No communication is a huge situation I encounter in companies.

We having discussed so many paths (it could actually take 2 weeks to literally get the real issue out but it always does)

So here was my client being demoted because they were too slow at the job.

Why were they?
Were they capable of doing the job? Yes
Could they go faster? Yes. So what was the problem?

In this case it was his perception of the Manager, who had got promoted before him and also his focus was on this every time he went to work.

Also the new manager was jokingly saying "I'm your boss now" which was really causing him such stress (we used the S+R=E Formula for this). He was not interested in turning up on time and doing the job to 100%, put this with the new software and it was affecting his sleep, diet and work and relationship.

I did this exercise on the Second week

ADULT

CHILD   **VICTIM**

You have 3 choices in life and work :-

The ADULT…………………………….Take control of your life and not blame others

THE VICTIM……………………….....Poor me (I have no luck everyone is out to get me)

THE CHILD .... Someone else can do that work, why should I do this?

His perception of his Manager was completely altered when we dissected the situation (when we discussed that his manager also had a boss to answer to and that was his job to get his teams to get the work complete each day. Had he related his situation to the Manager and explained how his comments were not beneficial or taken lightly on his behalf? (First of all I believe every Founder/Ceo/Manager should have a coach on how to treat staff in any given situation) Destructive feedback instead of constructive can destroy an employee and their energy to continue at their best.

Imagine if everyone decided to act like him?

We reversed roles and mirrored his situation. (Role play is a great way to dilute a situation and view it from the other person's perspective)
We discussed "A cost benefit analysis" (A coaching exercise) the advantages of staying or leaving and the disadvantages.

On our 3rd week he was building his self-discipline to work at 100% and not 50% which we found out having completed with him a "Work Profile" during our coaching sessions.

On our 4th week he was way happier in his job, turning up on time and totally even faster than his team mates. He was back chatting to the

Manager (sometimes Managers take a Leadership role and not use empathy for each team member's situation). It just took him longer to get used to the software. The discipline to decide to learn and practice was now there. Fear of new ways also is a problem.

The same guy is now Team Leader and has gone back to study a Business degree at UCC. He realised he was the Victim/Child profile instead of the Adult of his own life.

He had a high IQ but low EI before we started the coaching session to vice versa when leaving.

Also in this situation I do believe each company should look at their team's circadian rhythm and work around that. (discussed in an earlier chapter) Some people could work better early in the morning and others better later in the day.

Dale Carnegie was a great adviser on Employee self-esteem.

He discussed the ability of Charles Schwab's ability to deal and handle people. Schwab said the greatest asset any leader can have is to raise enthusiasm in your staff. How? Through appreciation and encouragement. He said there is nothing worse to kill a person's ambition than to criticise them.

"I have yet to find the man, however great or exalted his station, who did not do better work and put forth greater effort under a spirit of approval than he would ever do under a spirit of criticism"
Charles Schwab

You need to feed and nourish people's self esteem not your own as a leader.
Lillian Courtney

Discipline also helps your physical health and mental health.

NOTES:

DISCIPLINE

Reading one of Jim Kwik's books, he discussed the fact that we had 24 hours in a day. Yes we all know that but have we ever really looked into how much time we really have? Focused and disciplined, look how much we can actually get done.

Even myself now. I was chilling by the fire knowing I had to make lunches, iron clothes for the morning but was I disciplined? No, I kept putting it off until I thought of this book and jumped up and looked at the clock and gave myself an hour to do everything.

I had it completed within 40 minutes. You must shout and discipline yourself.

As a child you were told to do this and do that, your parents in most cases (having had my own children and now students) I see a change in different nationalities. The Irish mothers do everything, it is just the culture and the Italian mothers seem to be the same. Mine thank god are great cooks. Children find their way. Back to discipline so at 18 you are left to fend for yourself in the big bad world if you decide to leave the homestead. This is where Self-discipline comes in. No one to tell you to do this and that.

You must look at TIME in 3 sections. 8 +8+8=24

That is the norm for the world, Work+Off time+Sleep= 24

It is completely different for industries but let's just stick with the above scenario.

HOW TO STAY DISCIPLINED

8 hours to get up and prepare for the day.

A great tip is to arrange the night before a list of 2 or 3 things to get done hence when you wake up you are ready to go. Otherwise you will have that cup of coffee chill for a while then it's midday or end up confused and out of focus discipline is gone for the day. When people have work they have a routine. Get one going.

8 HRS

How are you spending your time if married you know it's probably collect children, drop, collect, lessons, meals, lunches and your time. If single, I just hope you are making use of every minute. This also means resting, you are still doing something when you rest, that is when your brain gets time to be creative. So many amazing inventors came up with ideas in the shower, when awaking, in a dream or out walking. So do not allow anyone to dismiss your rest and ME time.

8 HRS SLEEP

I wish I was disciplined with this. I am really trying hard and way better. than before. You make 4 chemicals in your brain between the hours of 9pm and 3amwhich are so important for your mind, body and soul. If you do not allow these chemicals to be produced you will head for dementia or something in later years. My son Adam as I discussed way above in the chapters brought to mind the dangers I was in due to my late nights and lack of sleep.

WHEN you sleep:-

It produced your natural chemicals that increases learning capacity and wait for it, it slows down ageing.

Also Melatonin and Serotonin are produced during 9pm and 3am.

Imagine what you are missing out on if you do not sleep.

We all know then that any left over thoughts, chemicals etc.. are cleaned out every night.

CHAPTER 11

SELF-VALUE

8.7

We are near the the end of our 8 S tool kit. Self value.   **URGENT**

I want you to go back now to the very beginning and check what number. you had put down on the value graph. Go back to page 37 on Value exercise.

1,000…………………..2,500…....................5,000

What did you say you would be sold for at a charity auction?

…................................. Old Value Number at the beginning

…................................. New Value Number at the end of reading thisbook.

I just hope you did this exercise at the beginning as you will get such benefit to see the huge change in yourself value.

Value your life as if it were a priceless Stone.

Below is **not my** story, it is a story that has 100's of time in life and insales and marketing colleges been used to discuss value. It was told to me during coaching training and also in one of the many books that I have read.

Value your life.

- A little boy went to his grandfather and asked him, "What is the value of life grandfather?"
- The grandfather gave him a stone and said, "First I want you to find out the value of this stone, but don't sell it."
- The boy took the stone to a fruit vendor and asked him what its value would be.
- The vendor saw the shiny stone and said, "How about you can take a dozen apples and give me the stone."
- The boy apologised and said that his grandfather had asked him not to sell it.

He went ahead and found a vegetable vendor.

- "What could be the value of this stone?" he asked the vegetable vendor.
- He saw the shiny stone and said, "How about you take a sack of potatoes and give me that stone."
- The boy again apologised and said he couldn't sell it.
- Further ahead, he went into a jewellery shop and asked the value of the stone.
- The jeweller saw the stone under a lens and said, "I will give you one million dollars for this stone."
- The boy was surprised, but explained that he couldn't sell the stone.
- Further ahead, the boy saw a large shop of precious stones and asked the value of this stone.
- When the precious stone shop owner was an expert in these matters. When he saw the stone, he lay down a cloth and put it on it.
- Then he walked in circles around the stone and bent down and scratched his head in front of it. "From where did you bring this priceless un cut diamond from?" he asked.

"Even if I sell everything I own, my whole shop, I won't be able to purchase this priceless diamond."

Stunned and confused, the boy returned to his grandfather and told him what had happened.

His grandfather said,

"The answers you got from the fruit vendor, the vegetable vendor, the jeweller and the precious stone's expert explain the value of our life. You may be a precious stone, even priceless, but, people will value you based on their own limited perceptions, beliefs, motives and expectations. How they value you says more about them than it does about you!

For this reason it is important to value yourself. Respect yourself. No longer indulge in meaningless comparisons with others. For you are unique, original and the only one of your kind in this universe. This is the value of your life.

Associate ever more with those who recognise your true value and ever less with those who see you just as a means to fulfil their own dreams and ambitions.
May you value the diamond in yourself and recognise the diamond in others as well.

Moral : We should treat people the way we want to be treated.

What is another moral of this story?

It is where you place yourself and how you value yourself that make the difference?
It is how you RESPECT yourself and what PRICE you put on your life or business.

In your life, who are you surrounding yourself with?

In business where are you placing your business for example pricing and valuing your work? Low end or high?

———

Thinking back on all the 8 S Toolkit now. I look and wonder if I had taken that scholarship for music at UCC where would I be now? Meeting Mr Linehan and being introduced to Psychology and Dr Norman Vincent Peale's works, how this changed the way my mind was thinking about life to positive and an opening vision to travel.

The one thing is I would never have worked in the Stock Exchange and got that amazing chance to have experienced the training and business of life. Lived in my own apartment in London. Neither would I have gone to France and lived there or had 3 wonderful children. It is so strange that one decision on the road ahead can change your life or works direction forever. I must say my life has been like most people, like the graph of a heart beat. We all have had ups and downs. It is to be prepared with the 8 S toolkit that will get you through the good and tsunami times of life. I look and feel gifted in the life I have.

All above really is to be Emotionally Intelligent.

We have our IQ but we have not been instructed on how to use our EI (Emotional Intelligence) The awareness to handle our emotions in any given situation.

A person with EI is far more intelligent than a person with high IQ. To be Emotionally Intelligent is the golden key to success. All 8 S's cover EI.

Life happens unexpectedly, move forward positively.

Why did I request you to start taking notes and writing?

It makes you think and remember, if not we as humans forget what we have read in an hours 50% in 24 hours ,70% and within a week.

I hope you can look back on each chapter and look at the notes you wrote in a few weeks time and keep going back to them to see the change and progress you are making.

Please do not waste the years of your life.

No purpose and pursuing nothing is a dangerous thing. This is such an uncomfortable place to be.

With no purpose one withdraws more. Hope comes from pursuit. One becomes anxious and lost in a fog of life and soullessness. (If there is such a word)

A positive emotion is built up by pursuing goals and meaning.

Harvard "grant" study covering 80 years of research resulted in realising longevity was not due to controlling blood pressure, glucose or cholesterol BUT the Quality of your relationships.

MY REPLY TO THIS RESEARCH.

I do believe when you are self aware, awake and emotionally intelligent you will never get bored on your own. (A relationship with yourself is more important to start with as you MUST BE your own best friend).

Once you are friends with yourself, you get on so well, sometimes you get too comfortable until you get out and meet friends, colleagues or family. Then you realise that it is so great to connect and learn from others (with like-minded people you can learn from).

I do believe this is essential to anyone working from home even 1 to 2 days per week to get to the office and to get out is so important for your health. Both physical and mental. We need people every now and then, for so many, others need people everyday. I am not like that. Even though I am an extrovert, I am also a deep introvert and need time on my own to bring peace and quiet to my mind. Also to get organised in my life or I cannot function. I am always organised in work having trained from Multinational companies from the beginning of my career and Secretarial college before I entered the workforce at an early age.

With children and being a parent it is so hard as you organise everyone around you and leave things for yourself last. (Unless you have plenty of money to get a nanny or help) there is no prefect parent or person so never forget that, most are a mess but this is a human thing trying to figure out so many areas in life.

I found this in my Moms notes after she died.

Nobody's family can hang out the sign "Nothing is the matter here"
Chinese proverb

Every home has its worries, troubles or grief at one time or another.

Every company has its ups and downs be prepared if you are a founder or an employee.

Congratulations once again you are a graduate of your own potential. Focused and successful.

I think we have come to the end of our journey together. It was so lovely and I will miss you all. I do believe you are a changed person even if you only got a few tips but hopefully you have learned something about yourself. Just before we leave I want you to write down your old story before you started my book. Now replace and write your new story to open up an amazing new life. Put on your carpenter tool kit (Coaching, ha ha sorry) and always have tools to handle any given situation especially with the tool belt.

S +R=E ....go back and find that tool it is just powerful and the golden ticket to success and peace of mind.

You must feel now a sense of achievement having got to this point of the book. Remember this is just not a book you throw away after finishing in the back of a shelf, it is a bedside bible for you to revisit. every time one of these S's seem to slip away.

One that I have kept until last.

Self love 8.8

'You live with yourself for 365 days a year and for the rest of your life. How do you treat yourself? What words do you use and say to yourself? Forgive yourself as God forgives you and as if building a muscle it takes time to put this into a habit of apologising to yourself and taking you out for nice surprises and having nice things and people around you. From today on begin to love YOU.

Congratulations once again you are a graduate of your own potential. Focused and successful.

So until we meet again, goodbye and look at the back of the book to contact with me and let me know how you are doing. As a gift for your hard work, throw me an email (lilliancourtneycoaching@gmail.com) and sign up for a complimentary 60 min coaching session, of course free of charge you having come this far.

Looking forward to hearing your amazing journey during our time together.

Your personal coach, Lillian

References from Client please Visit *"Google business Lillian Courtney Coaching"* Facebook Lillian Courtney Coaching etc…..

Please send me an email to let me know how you are getting along andI would love to hear a success story from the words of the book above having used the S' Tool-kit.

Coaching at the Dublin Chamber of Commerce as a Corporate Coach Consultant for The Irish Public Relations Academy introducing the benefits of Business & Personal coaching for corporates and SME's.

Student having completed my Personal Development Program at the College of Commerce in Cork. Ireland

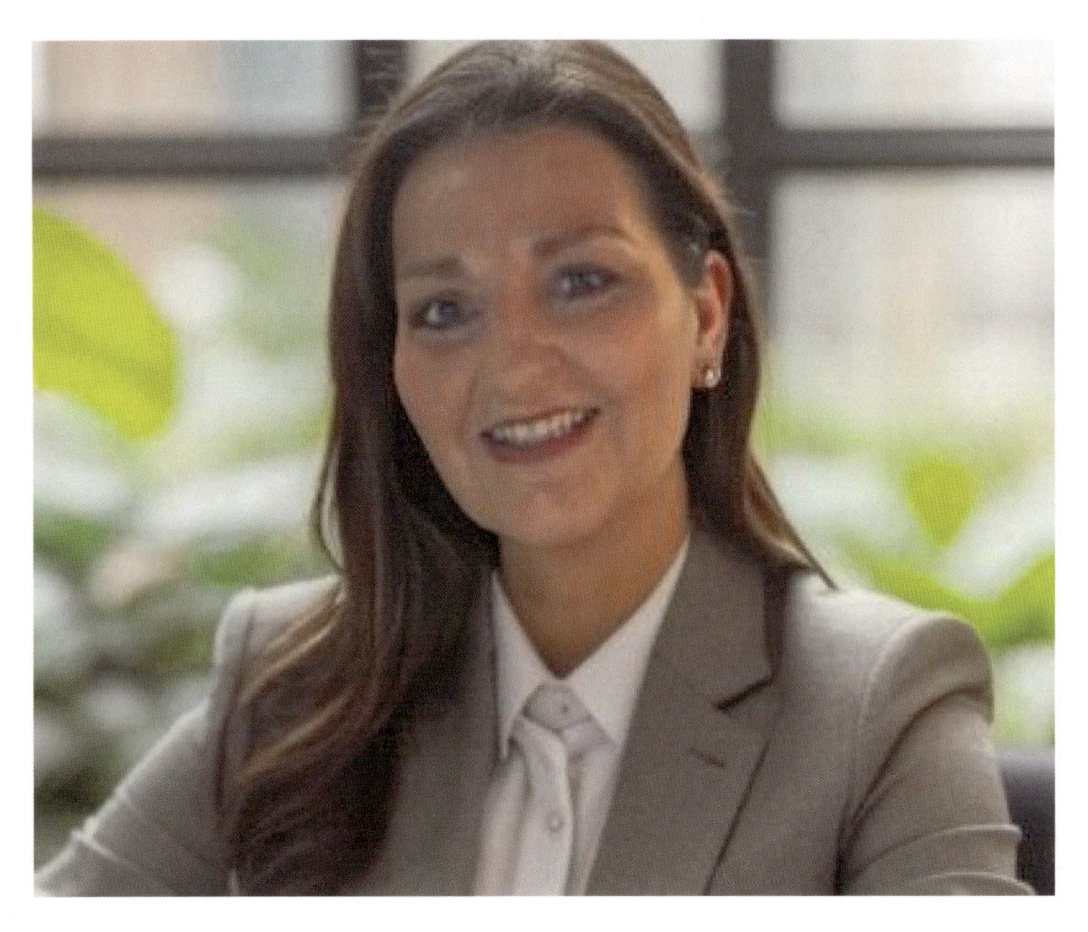

It was such a pleasure spending these past near 3 years with you all.

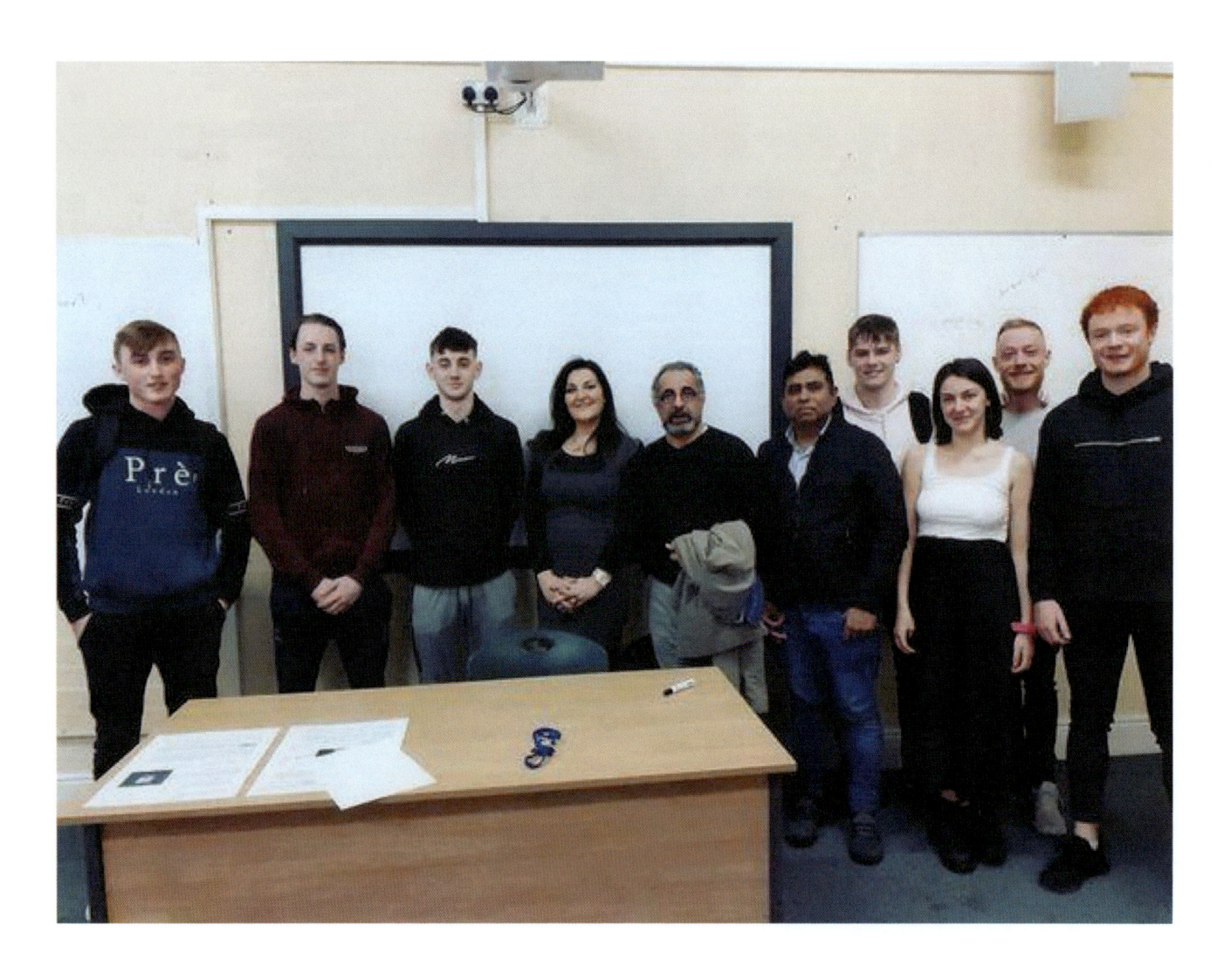

Giving a talk on my Personal Development Program to the Psychology Department at the College of Commerce to Staff and Students also on the benefits of Coaching combining Neuro coaching and the 8 S tool kit methodology.

Discussing the benefits of Design sprints combined with my coaching's toolkit methodology to UX and Graphic designers at the Bank of Ireland at my monthly Meetup group. This has built up to a monthly meetup group with different industries attending.

One of my Design sprint/Coaching training workshops using personal development and the 8 S toolkit.

One of 8 Company teams I Coached on Confidence and Tips for Public Speaking before giving their presentations in the Cork City Hall.

One of my Leadership creative confidence coaching workshopper facilitation workshops at the UNIVERSITY HOSPITAL,CORK 2023

I could go on with so many different photos of the different areas I cover in Business and Personal Coaching combining facilitation, design Sprints and NLP.

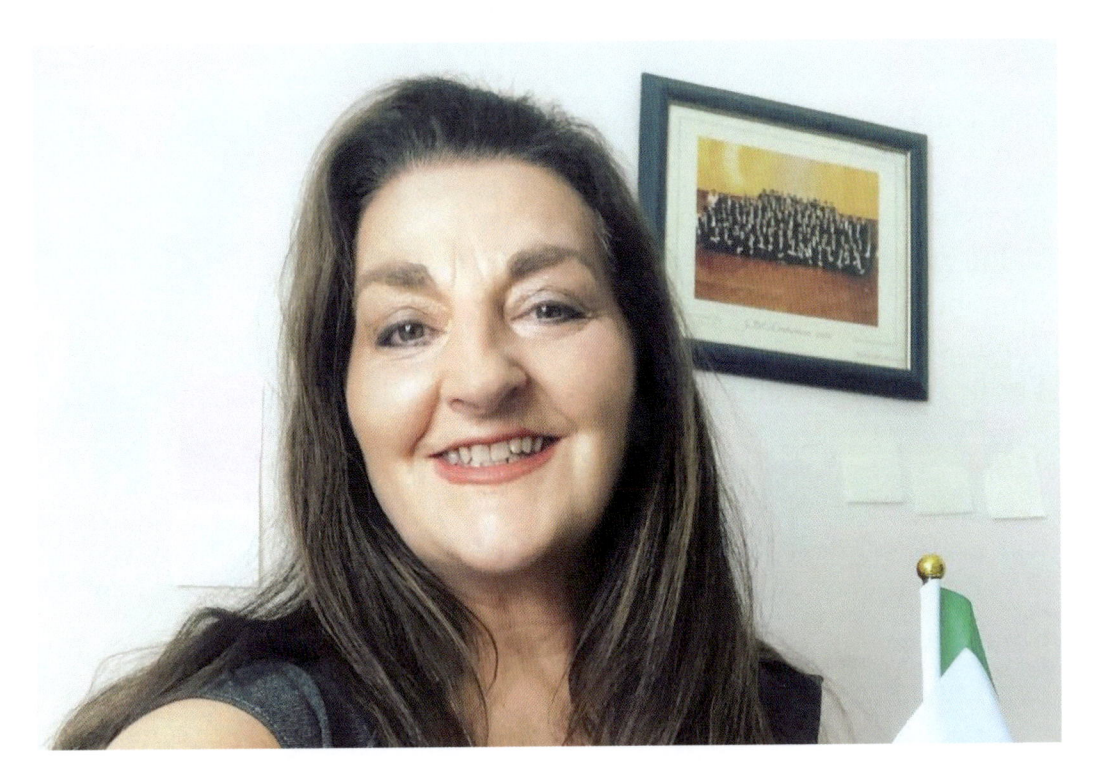

Please keep in contact and let me know how you like the book.

CONCLUSION

So here we are pumped up to 100% with Self Confidence, self value and Self Awareness and the rest of our 8 S toolkit, equipped to take on any given situation with your new methodology.

Look what you have learned. Let's summarise what we have learned.

- Layman's chat on how your brain functions
- Value graph exercise before reading. Write it here………..
- Mind body connection.
- Intelligence.
- The beginning to completion of the S toolkit.
- Final Value Graph. Write your answer here………………

No 2 and 6 are very important. If you completed the exercises correctly and read through the book you will see a great increase in your value number. If you began with a high number I hope and know you will take away great nuggets from this book.

If you need any further information please email me at
lilliancourtneycoaching@gmail.com
Add me on Instagram, Join me on LinkedIn.
Head over to Facebook Lillian Courtney Coaching for 100's of live videos

ABOUT THE AUTHOR

Lillian is a Corporate trainer, business & Personal Life coach /Master workshopper Facilitator/ Public Speaker and Communication trainer /Professional entertainer and musician

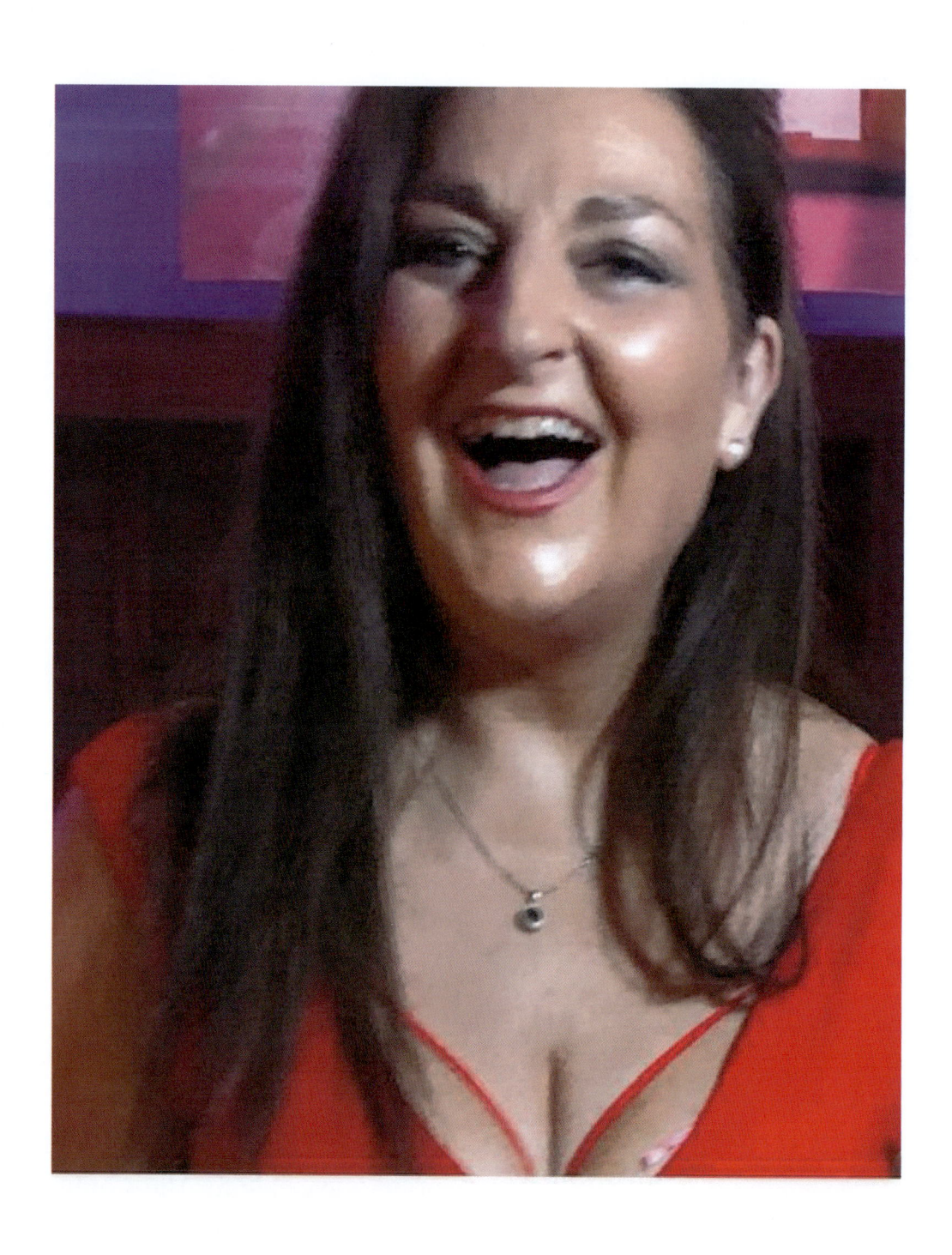

We are all responsible for our own happiness Do not let anyone make you feel responsible for their happiness. It is so hard as we as humans carry guilt around with us. Once you forgive or apologise to someone your subconscious mind lets go of that negative thought if you or that other person accept it as is. Otherwise you are living a life sentence if you do not let it go.

It was such a pleasure having spent such amazing time with you during this exciting journey also for myself. As this book has been in the writing cupboard of my mind for the past 10 to 15 years actually since the 80's. I would honestly love you to connect with me and let me know if any, if all of the 8 S tool kit helped you along the way.

Remember "Our deepest fear is not that we are inadequate, our deepest fear is that we are powerful beyond measure" Marianne Williamson.

Take these words away with you and live the life you deserve and meant to live.

Yes, we have completed this book together. I thank you for joining me on this amazing journey.

Do not forget to keep in contact with me. I would love to hear your success stories.

Psalm 23.3 and Scene 1 of Hamlet "To thine own self be true"
Take these last words away with you.

Coach Lil xx

Here I am again saying will I add my recent workshops and seminar photos. Good bye all see you hopefully at one of my workshops or online. Keep in CONTACT.

BOOK REFERENCE:

DR NORMAN VINCENT PEALE.: THE POWER OF POSITIVE THINKING
JIM KWICK: LIMITLESS
SHONTE JOVANDE TAYLOR: GEN X
DON MIGUEL RUIZ: THE 4 AGREEMENTS
STEVEN COVEY: THE 7 HABITS OF SUCCESS PEOPLE
RESEARCH: GOOGLE
NOTES: BUSINESS & PERSONAL COACH ILI/ICF
NOTES: NEUROSCIENCE AND PSYCHOLOGY.

Printed in Great Britain
by Amazon